THE CHURCH PLANTER'S TRAINING MANUAL

THE CHURCH PLANTER'S TRAINING MANUAL

Fred G. King

CHRISTIAN PUBLICATIONS
CAMP HILL, PENNSYLVANIA

Christian Publications
3825 Hartzdale Drive, Camp Hill, PA 17011

The mark of  vibrant faith

ISBN: 0-87509-526-7
LOC Catalog Card Number: 92-74653
©1992 by Christian Publications
All rights reserved
Printed in the United States of America

92 93 94 95 96 5 4 3 2 1

The publishers would like to thank:

Discovery Publishing, the publications ministry of Peninsula Bible Church, Palo Alto,
CA for permission to use "God's Spec Sheet for Church Leaders" by Bob Smith.

Dr. W.A. Criswell, for permission to quote him in "The Preacher in His Study."

CONTENTS

ACKNOWLEDGMENTS

It is with deepest gratitude that we acknowledge the following individuals for their contribution to *The Church Planter's Training Manual*:

Rev. Richard Bailey

Rev. Daryl Dale

Rev. Dennis Gorton

Rev. Paul Radford

Rev. John Sawin

Patti Scott Sellers
Administrative Staff Assistant
Office of Church Growth

Linda Wood
Cover Design
Office of Church Growth

Joan Wicks
Secretary
Office of Church Growth

PUBLISHER'S INTRODUCTION

Missions, evangelism and the planting of churches have always been the heart of The Christian and Missionary Alliance. Because of this heartbeat, the Alliance, from its founding by Dr. A.B. Simpson over 100 years ago, to the present day, has always been willing to work with other churches, para-church organizations and individual believers who proclaim the name of Jesus Christ. It is in that spirit of cooperation that *The Church Planter's Training Manual* is presented to the evangelical church at large.

Why should the evangelical church take notice? Because since 1977, the Alliance has been one of the fastest growing evangelical denominations year after year. Between 1977 and its centennial in 1987, the Alliance constituency more than doubled in size. Its innovations in missions are studied in many seminaries as models for others to follow.

The planting of churches is central to Alliance growth strategies and success. It is out of a program started in 1987, *1000 more by 94*, that this manual comes. Developed by Church Growth Director Fred King, himself an expert from the trenches with four successful church plants under his belt, this manual provides practical information to pastors, churches and denominations who desire to plant churches.

While it was originally written for Alliance churches—as you will see in some sections—the material in *The Church Planter's Training Manual* can be adapted to any situation and group. You may feel free to copy or adjust any of the forms to suit your needs.

Above all, our desire is to see lost people come to Christ, and His Body, the Church, built up.

PREFACE

Manuals, books, tapes, videos and other helps fill our bookshelves—all with claims as to how-to-do-it. The apostle John said, "Jesus did many other things as well. If every one of them were written down, I suppose that even the whole world would not have room for the books that would be written" (John 21:25). This is how many of us feel about the subject of church growth and church planting.

This manual, although very practical in its approach to planting a new church, cannot replace that which God has already provided for us in written form, the Word of God. Church Planting Directors, although experts in church planting, cannot replace the Church Planter—the Holy Spirit of God!

Personally, I like the apostle Paul's advice to Timothy, "In the presence of God and of Christ Jesus, who will judge the living and the dead, and in view of his appearing and his kingdom, I give you this charge: *Preach the Word*" (2 Timothy 4:1-2a, italics added).

Doesn't that say it all? Preach the Word! You may do everything "right," but if you fail to "preach the Word," you fail! Now that requires prayer—concerted, protracted, continual prayer. The healthy, growing, evangelistic church is known for its prayer and preaching.

Yes, use this manual. Absorb its very practical contents. But above all, pray and preach the Word and God will abundantly bless you and His church! Again, preach the Word when it is convenient and when it is not. It is our prayer that God's continual blessing will be on you, faithful church planter.

Fred G. King
National Director of Church Growth
The Christian and Missionary Alliance

Purpose

The purpose of this manual is to provide the church planter and local church with a practical working tool on how to start a new church.

CHAPTER 1

The Theology of Church Planting

THE IMPORTANCE OF CHURCH PLANTING

By Richard Bailey

A FRESH REVELATION

Someone once said, "The church is the ultimate goal of the universe and so far as revelation is concerned the solitary reason for creation." The evangelical community has a poor understanding of ecclesiology. Spiritless worship, lack of corporate prayer, prejudices within the assembly and ineffective witness all point to a church that has lost a clear focus of its spiritual life. We desperately need a fresh revelation of the church glorious!

CHRIST—THE LIFE OF HIS CHURCH

The Church was purchased by the blood of Christ. When Christ was raised from the dead, it was to ascend as Head of all things to the Church. The Church is likened to His body. It is the Church that Christ loves, honors and protects. When He comes again it is to rapture His Church. The one unique element of the Church that cannot be duplicated by any other institution is its life. That life is the very life of Christ. It is this element of life that must be understood.

REPRODUCTION—ESSENTIAL TO LIFE

Aristotle said, "All things are said to be alive which determine themselves to movement or operation of any kind." The biologist tells us that the unique features of life necessitate three ingredients: (1) growth, (2) nourishment, (3) reproduction. Growth takes place by regeneration or the replacement of another part. It is also possible for cells to change in size by their growth. Nourishment is essential to life as no living thing can exist apart from energy; it is energy that makes possible mobility of mind and body. Reproduction is the process whereby living things produce more of their own kind. This is possible through the dividing of cells or by germination. Every living thing must nourish itself, must grow and must reproduce. This is the minimum, not the maximum, function of organic life.

THE CHURCH—A LIVING ORGANISM

When we confess that the Church is the Body of Christ we are in fact saying that the Church is a living organism. As a living organism she is not exempt from the principle of life which necessitates growth, nourishment and reproduction.

GOD'S WILL

The hope of the Church rests not in maturity but rather in our ability to reproduce after our kind. We must always remember that it is God's will that we be fruitful and multiply.

MULTIPLICATION

The record of the apostolic church was one of reproduction by division, brought about through the dispersion. It also reproduced by germination through planting the gospel seed throughout Asia. It all began with 120 believers; then 3,000, then 5,000, then multitudes believed. And in Acts 9 we read of two whole towns responding to the gospel.

It was not long, however, until institutionalism took over and by the year A.D. 325 the Church had substituted structure and organization for the life-giving principle of reproduction. In place of growth, the Church became molded into the Roman government and ultimately fell prey to state religion. The Church, now well organized and with political clout, became sterile until the mighty Reformation took place in the 1500s. This same pattern has been duplicated in denominations and local churches.

LIVE BY GIVING LIFE TO ANOTHER

The Church of Jesus Christ must reproduce. There is no other way to continue life except by reproduction. Both my grandfather and father have died; however, their life is continued through their children's children. Had my grandfather not had any children, some 130 persons would not be living today.

This same principle is true of the church. Where are the 100-year-old church congregations? Pastors have gone, congregations have changed, and most of the buildings that housed them are extinct. Isaiah said it clearly, "Their stock shall not take root in the earth" (40:24, KJV). The Church lives only by giving its life to another, either by dividing and planting its life in another community or by taking the gospel to another community and planting the seed of life.

"I WILL BUILD MY CHURCH"

A recent survey indicated that in the United States the average city of 50,000 people has approximately 100 churches. If we assume 300 people will be in attendance next Sunday in each of these 100 churches, we must also assume that 20,000 people will not attend church in that city. There are unreached people for whom Christ died in every city of North America and the world. We must go into every community with this glorious gospel of salvation. Christ loves the church, and as we put ourselves in the way of planting, He has promised, "I will build my church."

THE CALL OF THE CHURCH PLANTER

Many denominations are committed to church planting. We have witnessed a wonderful forward momentum, yet there have been some church-planting failures. Many reasons for the successes and failures could be noted. The pastor who is a successful church planter possesses the following:

- A clear call from God.
- A strong personal prayer life.
- A powerful expository preaching ministry.
- A proper understanding of spiritual gifts.
- Thorough evangelistic training in church growth and church planting.

A CLEAR CALL FROM GOD

The church planter is a called-out man of God. God has set him apart for full-time Christian work. God's call goes beyond the obedient response to Scripture; it is a special experience that only those God has uniquely separated out have received. God's call goes beyond the obedient response of every believer to be a faithful witness to the lost. That is something we are all to do.

The call of God on a man to full-time Christian work begins with a powerful compulsion from God to serve our Lord Jesus with all of his heart, soul, spirit and body. He has no other choice. When asked if he can do or would like to do anything else if it were at all possible, his immediate response is, "I must serve Jesus. I cannot and will not do anything else."

Connected with this powerful compulsion is the person's will. He has given it over to the Lord and he desires to do nothing else with his time other than to serve Jesus, his Lord. He will go anywhere under any circumstances in order to preach Christ. When God has separated out a man of His choosing there will be very clear and specific results. He will be a soul-winner. People will come to Christ as a result of his ministry. Jesus said, "You did not choose me, but I chose you and appointed you to go and bear fruit—fruit that will last. Then the Father will give you whatever you ask in my name" (John 15:16).

A STRONG PERSONAL PRAYER LIFE

Prayer is the vital ingredient to any ministry, but without a doubt the church planter's personal prayer life will make the difference between whether a church is established on the basis of man-made programs or resting in the direction of the Head of the Church, Jesus Christ our Lord.

A leader who early-on establishes a personal prayer life will soon begin corporate prayer with church leaders. This will soon radiate out to the congregation.

When the church leaders devote sacrificial prayer time to the Lord, He will cause miraculous things to occur. Daily early morning prayer with church leaders must not be construed as a "magic trick" to cause growth. On the contrary, when we pray and commit every step to the Lord, He brings the increase. He becomes our total supply, our resource.

A POWERFUL EXPOSITORY PREACHING MINISTRY

Some have contended that the day of expository preaching is gone. This is a frightening thought. The emphasis today on topical preaching designed to appeal to the non-Christian could very well signal the demise of the evangelical movement of the past 200 years.

Although non-Christians must be urged and invited to come to church, it is most dangerous to preach only to the unsaved. The Church is the assembly of believers during which the whole counsel of the Word of God must be declared—declared in such a way

7

that the people of the Church will be equipped and mobilized to be His witnesses where they live, work and play.

Elements of the church growth movement have unwittingly undermined the very heart of that which builds a strong and growing church. Focusing primarily on the "unchurched," while sounding correct, is not the Church's first priority. Its first priority must be "to prepare God's people for works of service" (Ephesians 4:12). The result will be the "upbuilding" or growth of the church. This must be accomplished through expository preaching and teaching.

A PROPER UNDERSTANDING OF SPIRITUAL GIFTS

The majority of pastors have at least a basic knowledge and understanding of the spiritual gifts. Tragically, however, it would seem that few have grasped the incredible importance of properly discovering and exercising the gifts.

Some will say it takes no spiritual gift to plant churches. If that is the case then few churches will ever be started. On the contrary, a church planter is, in the opinion of this writer, a manifestation of the multifaceted spiritual gifts of pastor-teacher (Ephesians 4:11), as well as of evangelist.

Not only must the church planter be called of God and be gifted for this special ministry, he must also be committed to teaching his people the spiritual gifts. There is included in this book a special segment on the spiritual gifts and how to structure the church accordingly.

THOROUGH EVANGELISTIC TRAINING IN CHURCH GROWTH AND CHURCH PLANTING

Over the years many have gone forth to proclaim Christ to those who have never heard (Romans 15:20) and have experienced great success. Others have gone forth with the same call, desire and fervor to reach the lost and plant churches, yet have struggled and experienced failure. How can this happen? Their calling was clear. Their gifts were proper. Their motives were wonderful. The need was great. The opportunity obviously was there. What happened? Again, many things can be listed as possibilities, but perhaps the problem would lay in the lack of proper training for the special ministry of church planting.

Few Bible and seminary graduates are specifically trained in how to start a successful church. Some receive a few courses on church growth principles, but rarely on specific methodologies. This is why special training in church planting, growth and evangelism is essential. Intensive training provides the church planter with the tools to start a successful church. Experienced pastors, recent graduates, missionaries and leading laymen will all benefit from training in these three areas. Today, most evangelical denominations either provide helps or recommend organizations which do.

Perhaps with helps of this caliber the success rate and quality of new churches will be dramatically improved.

SERVING TOGETHER—PROCEDURAL MATTERS WHEN WORKING WITH A DENOMINATION OR "MOTHER" CHURCH

While many of you who feel called to church planting may be independent of a denomination, there are very real advantages to being associated with a group—be it either a denomination or a large "mother" church that wishes to plant "daughter" congregations. This section discusses the relationship and its importance.

LICENSING

Extension pastors must be licensed official workers in the denomination. The established guidelines and requirements of the current manual of the denomination and the bylaws of the respective district must be carefully examined and followed.

WORKING RELATIONSHIPS

If an established church plans to parent a new church, the pastor and the church governing board must first seek approval of those in authority over them. Do not proceed without this authorization for, among others, the following reasons:

1. To be certain that denominational policies and requirements are followed.
2. To be certain that those individuals desiring to start the new church understand and are in complete sympathy with the distinctives of the denomination.
3. To be certain that a pastor or lay leader is not appointed or called outside of the established procedures.
4. To be certain that the giving to denominational church planting by the parent church will not be affected in the planting of a daughter church; i.e., the parent church must continue its faithful giving to church planting in that if it were reduced or withdrawn other new churches, pastors and funded programs could be endangered as well as giving to overseas missions.
5. To be certain that the leaders of both the parent church and the daughter church have thoroughly studied this manual with those in authority over them in order to insure an efficient church-planting process.
6. To be certain that the senior pastor of the parent church and the church-planting pastor of the new church have both attended specialized training in church planting and growth.
7. To be certain that the church-planting pastor has received evangelism training to insure thorough training and experience in soul-winning.
8. To be certain that both the parent and daughter church understand and agree to constituted authority in that the new church is under the direct

authority of those over them and that there will be a spirit of unity and cooperation among all three.

9. To be certain that premature decisions, such as property and/or building purchase or construction; large expenditures; the hiring or calling of staff without proper credentials and denominational approval does not occur.

QUALITIES OF A CHURCH PLANTER

The following qualities are listed as "preferred" and "must." Church growth leaders over the years have noted these qualities and characteristics in the most successful church planters. Perhaps the denomination's Church Growth Director, the prospective church planter and the core group should consider these qualities as they look for God's man in the pastoral selection process.

PREFERRED QUALITIES

1. Outgoing personality. He likes people and people like him. He smiles often.
2. A self-starter/motivator.
3. A visionary. Positive thinker. Imaginative and creative.
4. Excellent health and vigor.
5. Presents nice public appearance—grooming, clothing.
6. A graduate of Bible college or seminary.

NECESSARY QUALITIES

1. A commitment to a personal daily prayer life.
2. A desire to excel in preaching. He must *love* to preach!
3. A deep commitment to the denomination and its distinctives.
4. Thoroughly trained in church planting, church growth and evangelism.
5. Experienced in pastoral service either as an assistant, associate or senior pastor. Flexibility is somewhat allowed.
6. A history of soul winning is essential.
7. Called of God to plant churches.
8. A visionary, a man of faith.
9. A hard worker, self-motivator, overcomer of obstacles.
10. Maintains a strong, regular daily prayer life which will involve the men of the new church.
11. Committed to constituted authority. He will be amenable to those over him in the Lord.
12. He will submit regular progress reports as required.
13. He will give strong pastoral leadership to the new church.

14. He will be involved in one or more evangelistic outreaches to the unchurched community.
15. He will train and disciple his people.
16. He will lead his church in parenting other churches.

GOOD QUESTIONS FOR A CHURCH PLANTER

The following questions are intended to be thought-provoking. Please use them in a positive way to stimulate creative thinking which will enhance your ministry. It is recommended that you write out your answers to these questions. Church committees and boards may copy these questions for candidate interviews.

1. Why are you or why do you want to be an extension pastor?

2. Write out in clear specifics in outline form how you would start a new church. Develop your strategy in logical sequence.

3. Specify why you are positive that a church will grow in the area which you have selected.

4. Identify the cultural characteristics of your area.

5. What are the five most common occupations in your area?

6. What is the average income for the average family in your area?

7. What is the average educational level of the people in your area?

8. How many people in your area go to church regularly (any church)?

9. How many homes are for sale in your area?

10. What is the average selling price?

11. How many new families have moved into your area in the last 12 months?

12. What are the three greatest felt needs of your area?

13. What are you doing to meet those needs?

14. How many adults have you prayed with to receive Christ during the past 12 months?

15. How many new Christian adults have you baptized during the past 12 months?

16. How specifically do you train your people in evangelism?

17. How specifically do you equip your people as disciples?

18. How many unchurched people live within a 20-minute drive of your church?

19. What features of your worship service will cause visitors to want to come back?

20. Are your messages geared to Christians or non-Christians?

21. How far in advance do you plan and work on your messages?

22. How many hours do you put into sermon preparation?

23. How much time weekly do you pray over your message?

24. How many times do you practice-preach your message?

25. Are your messages practical?

26. Can a 12-year-old understand and respond to your preaching?

27. Do you smile when you preach? Are you sure?

28. Are you a good preacher? How do you know?

29. Listen to three tapes of your preaching. Are you a good preacher?

30. How far in advance do you plan and prepare for special music in your worship service?

31. What style of Christian music does your congregation enjoy? How do you know?

32. What are the most attractive features about the morning worship service?

33. If I visited your church and I brought a 15-month-old child, would I want to leave the child in your nursery or toddlers' room?

34. How many visitors during the last 12 months came back for the second time?

35. How many visitors during the last 12 months have made this their church home?

36. How do you use the church people in the worship service?

37. Why would I want to come to your church?

38. Why would my elementary-age children want to come to your church?

39. Why would my teenage children want to come to your church?

40. Why would college-age people want to come to your church?

41. Why would middle-age adults want to come to your church?

42. How would a visitor see the facility, inside and out?

43. How would a visitor like the looks of the bulletin and other church literature?

44. You are a model for your people. How does your congregation reflect you?

45. What is the percentage of growth in your church over the past 12 months?

46. What is the actual numerical growth over the past 12 months?

48. How many new people were already Christians when they began attending?

49. How many new people became Christians through your ministry during the past year?

50. What is the major reason for no-growth in your church?

CHAPTER 2

The Church Planter's Personal Life

FAMILY

All too often we hear of pastors who have neglected their families as they built the church. It is unfortunate that this happens. An exciting and dynamic new church has been established, but a lovely wife and children have been left to fend for themselves as Dad has gone out to build the kingdom.

Perhaps this is one of the key reasons for teaching time management. There is so very much to accomplish but seemingly not enough time. Not true! God has given us all the time He wants us to have and not a minute more. That means there really is the proper amount of time for the pastor's wife and his children. A pastor must develop his priorities biblically, write them out and implement a daily, weekly, monthly and yearly working schedule. This schedule must include proper daily and weekly quality time for his family. This time must be purposely built-in and faithfully followed. In addition, the pastor must write in his yearly vacation schedule.

The success of the pastor is directly related to the love, concern, attention and support he gives to his wife. After all, God created marriage, the family and the home long before He created the Church! As the pastor carefully protects his wife and children he will be happily surprised at how well the church goes!

Also the pastor must carefully guard his health. Preachers are noted for early heart attacks and other related problems. A regulated diet and exercise program will add years to his life and life to his years!

PERSONAL FINANCES

Church planting is not the most financially lucrative ministry, but many will say it is the most spiritually rewarding. The new pastor often finds himself in difficult financial straits yet expressing confidence, enthusiasm and trust in the all-sufficiency of God which frequently shines like a light in a dark place.

PERSONAL BUDGET

BIBLICAL INSTRUCTION

God expects us to be wise stewards and to provide for our family but also to set a faith-example for the new church people. This requires the pastor to give thorough biblical instruction which he has learned by personal practice.

SUBSIDY

Often a church planter may receive partial subsidy from his denomination as well as private gifts. He must guard against becoming overly dependent on these temporary funds. One day they will cease. There are known cases where, due to outside support, the pastor and church were lax in their goal of becoming self-supporting. Often, it seems that when all is well financially, correspondingly the rate of church growth slows.

When the district establishes a declining scale of subsidy, it becomes apparent that either church growth must occur or soon the pastor will not have adequate support.

PUTTING IN THE TIME

Although the pastor may have a short-term commitment due to a missionary candidacy status, it is so very important that he faithfully give all his energies to developing the ministries of the church. We recommend a minimum three-year commitment. Of course a long-term commitment is much more necessary if the church is to be self-supporting.

CHURCH GROWTH

The answer to proper pastoral support is church growth. It is the direct responsibility of the pastor to see that growth and financial stability do occur. Church planting and church growth are hard work, but they are rewarding work resulting in a soul-winning church!

SUGGESTED BUDGET

It is well worth your time to write out your personal budget. Keep it with your checkbook and stay within its framework. Without a budget many pastors' families end up in debt. All too many marriages suffer greatly due to financial problems. This is a suggested guide in developing your personal budget:

(1) Tithe - 10 percent
(2) Savings - 10 percent
(3) House - 25 percent
(4) Utilities - 5 percent
(5) 50 percent for:
   • food and entertainment
   • auto
   • clothing
   • taxes
   • insurance - health, life, auto
   • education
   • miscellaneous

LIVING CONDITIONS
THE PARSONAGE

Closely related to the church planter's personal finances is his living conditions. Frequently because of his income level he must rent an apartment or house that is not only too small for his family but adequate for entertaining only a few people at a time. What can be done?

DO NOT RENT TOO QUICKLY

Although inconvenient, it is recommended that the pastor spend a considerable amount of time searching for a house that is not only suitable for his family but also large enough and properly located in order to entertain, conduct home Bible studies and various special meetings.

GOD WILL PROVIDE

As you pray God will begin to give you an abundance of leads to examine. It is okay to write down the amenities needed, including your maximum rental amount. For example:

Location
- section of community you desire
- neighborhood characteristics
- kind of schools needed
- shopping
- near the church's temporary meeting place

Home
- the physical condition, inside and out
- floor plan - room layout, number of bedrooms and size
- insulation, heating, utilities
- draperies, curtains, carpeting
- plumbing and number of baths

You should make this a family project so that, when God provides the house, together you can thank Him.

UPKEEP OF THE PARSONAGE

The pastor and his family are the most visible of all church families. Although they prefer to blend in like any other family, that is not possible. The pastor, his family and their home are a testimony to all.

- Maintain the exterior of the house even though, and especially because, it is rented. Keep the windows and doors clean and in good repair.

- If the house needs paint or repair, perhaps the owner would exchange a nice paint job for a month's rent. Ask him!

- Not only should you maintain the lawn, try to improve it.

- Keep the house clean inside. Using good judgment on cleanliness is of great importance. Not only do you set a fine example for your children, but your home becomes a testimony to your landlord, neighborhood and the church people.

LEASING A HOME

Most landlords use a standard lease/rental form. Be sure to read it carefully and take note of any unusual contingencies. Do not lock yourself in too tightly. There could come a time when a move would be necessary. Most owners require a one-year lease with a one-month security clearing deposit. With the owner, walk through the house and around the exterior. Write down any damage or conditions you can find. You must not be held accountable for existing problems. You could be, it you fail to note them on the lease agreement. Often stationary or office supply stores carry sample rental and lease forms. It would be good to familiarize yourself with these before signing a copy. Be certain to coordinate with your denomination's extension director or superintendent or your sponsoring church's board to avoid pitfalls.

PRAYER AND DEVOTIONAL LIFE

A pastor's daily walk with God is undoubtedly the most important aspect of his life and ministry. The quality of time spent alone with God as well as in the reading of His Word will shape and mold every aspect of his personal and family life. How can the man of God effectively minister to his flock if he himself has not been ministered to by God's Spirit?

DETERMINE TO DISCIPLINE

The Priority of Prayer

It would be wise to work prayerfully through the things which are of greatest importance to you. Make a list, then begin to adjust until you arrive at an order which you believe is honoring to God. An example would be:

A private, personal prayer time.
"Very early in the morning, while it was still dark, Jesus got up, left the house and went off to a solitary place, where he prayed" (Mark 1:35).

What are the elements here?

"Very early in the morning." This should be a priority. It is the quietest time of the day, and chances are slim that you will be interrupted. Obviously this time may not be the best for some. However, a commitment of a special time should be set aside.

"Jesus got up, left the house and went off to a solitary place." It may not be necessary to actually leave the house, but sometimes it is, to be certain you can be totally alone with God. Trying to lie in bed to pray or sitting in the living room with a cup of coffee does not necessarily speak of discipline or sacrifice. Jesus did something that was not convenient. Perhaps we should consider sacrificing comfort and convenience in order to be alone with God.

"Where he prayed." This is the incarnate Son of God who is going to pray! Think on that for a moment. If Jesus our Lord demonstrated the need to pray, to be alone with the Father, how much more should we be certain to be alone with God?

The Priority of God's Word

In conjunction with your daily prayer time, read God's Word. He will give you clear direction for the day as you read. He will provide answers to prayer as you read. But above all the reading and praying, as you read, God's Word will bring about a wonderful and special worship experience early in the morning.

DETERMINE TO ACT

As you meet with God each morning and read His Word, something quite remarkable will begin to occur. You will discover that you cannot pray and read the Word of God without being motivated by the Holy Spirit to take action. It could be a witnessing and soul-winning desire. It could be the opening of an entirely new avenue of ministry. It could be coming to the rescue of a hurting person. You will find that not only will your head and heart be affected, your hands and feet will need to move out for God. No longer will you be content with another non-active day—you will be determined to act in the power of God's Spirit.

Your prayer and devotional life will no longer be hit-and-miss. It will not be boring and lifeless. Rather your entire life will be filled with enthusiasm from God!

PERSONAL APPEARANCE

GROOMING

The way we dress and groom ourselves is a direct reflection of our attitude toward our calling as pastors. This is not to say that every pastor can afford expensive suits, shirts, ties and shoes, or the latest in hairstyling, but a pastor can be certain that he is neatly clothed with hair trimmed, combed and shoes shined. In the business world, the military and most institutions today, the leaders and employees present a sharp appearance to their clientele and the world around. Should not those representing the King as His personal ambassadors strive to present themselves as professionally as possible?

CULTURAL SENSITIVITY

A pastor must be sensitive to the culture in which he lives. Simply because it is a rural area does not necessarily mean he should wear Levis, except when appropriate for a special activity. In warmer climates the accepted dress may be sport shirts. However, he should check with the established pastors of the area before deciding what is or is not proper. The use of good judgment and the desire to present a strong testimony even by personal appearance is of utmost importance.

Above all, always smile!

DEVELOPING RELATIONSHIPS

It is not uncommon to learn that a pastor has experienced difficulties in developing strong, personal relationships with not only church people but also those unchurched to which he is committed to reach with the good news.

IDENTIFY WITH THE CHURCH PEOPLE

Get to Know Them

It is difficult, if not impossible, for a pastor to really appreciate his people if he fails to get to know them. Now this is not to say that he should get to know every person in the congregation, especially if the church is committed to becoming a multi-cell body of believers. However, he must be highly visible to the people. Participating in work days, recreational events, church outings and special projects are a few of the things he should do to get to know his people.

Have Fun with the Leaders

Activities with the individual members of the church governing board, such as jogging, handball, hunting or fishing, will develop a bond of friendship that will transfer out to the entire congregation as the leaders speak of the personal warmth and concern of their pastor.

Do Not Hide Out

Some pastors isolate themselves from their people under the guise of study and an authoritarian attitude. Although the proper disciplines of study and attention to necessary administrative detail are very important, identifying with the people and especially the church leaders is also critically important.

IDENTIFY WITH THE UNCHURCHED

The pastor must become the example and model of evangelism for his people or his finely honed sermon will fall on deaf ears. In other words, he must practice what he preaches. If he insists on the people being soul winners, he must be able to present current personal-experience testimony about souls won.

Get Involved in the Community

A wise pastor will become the friend of the community leaders. The mayor, councilmen, chief of police and leading community service groups are just a few avenues which he should consider.

The police chaplaincy is strongly recommended because it immediately places the pastor into a community leadership position. In addition, he has ample opportunities to share Christ with people in crisis.

Become Visible

The pastor should sponsor or help with as many community events as possible, although he may not personally be involved—the Boy Scouts, sports activities, voting booths and so on. Be creative and always be on the lookout for opportunities to become known and present the gospel to those who otherwise would not normally visit the church. Here are a few ideas:

- Chamber of Commerce
- Little League
- Mayor's prayer breakfast
- Businessmen's organizations
- Various community celebrations

CHAPTER 3

How to Plant a Church

FORMING THE INITIAL CORE GROUP

This is perhaps the most important subject to the new church planter. He may have abundant information on how to grow a church, develop a multitude of important ministries and even be a gifted preacher and Bible teacher, but initially he wants to know, "Where do I find the first core of committed Christians who will be my support group and ministry team?" Until he has an answer for this he will not be satisfied with any other subject.

We should note that the church group is simply the initial core of Christians who are committed to seeing a new church started in their community.

From where do the church group people come? There are many sources; here are a few:

THE PARENT-CHURCH METHOD

A DESIRE

A parent or mother church is an established church which is led of God to plant a daughter church in its community or neighboring town. God has placed a desire within the group to reach its neighbors for Jesus Christ. As an expression of this, the church prayerfully makes a commitment to plant an evangelistic church.

A BIBLE STUDY

Often they will begin this outreach by starting a Bible study in the target area or community. Sometimes the study is led by a layman who is trained in evangelism and Bible teaching. Frequently a staff pastor or even the senior pastor develops the study. Regardless of who leads, the vision is implemented by the church body agreeing together that this is in obedience to the Great Commission.

MISSION TEAM

Usually a group of committed believers from the parent church will either temporarily, or in some cases permanently, go as the founding church group, and thus provide the new work with mature Christians who know their spiritual gifts and are eager to be a part of this mission team.

A FINANCIAL COMMITMENT

In addition, the church group will also commit their tithes and offerings to the new work. This is essential for a healthy church start. Also, the parent church usually will place in their budget an amount to assist the daughter church for a specified period of time.

GETTING STARTED

Getting started in becoming a parent church is up to the pastor. Nothing succeeds in a church without his support. The following list will give ideas of how to launch a church in this cooperative effort to make church planting a logical and natural function of the local church.

- *Be determined to involve your church in the "Churches Planting Churches" concept.* It is impossible to overestimate the importance of the leadership and support of a Spirit-filled pastor. If you are committed and enthusiastic, your people will catch your spirit and will become involved.

- *Be personally in tune with and supportive of your denomination's plan for church planting.* Your church should be involved in planting other churches in your own community and at the same time be fully supportive of the overall denomination's program. Remember there are 190 million lost people in the United States, and we can do something about it!

- *Preach or teach the New Testament theology of churches planting churches.* If your congregation understands the biblical concepts, they will become more interested in the need to plant other churches in your community.

- *Set tentative goals as to how many churches your church will plant.* Report this number to the denomination so they can include your goal with the other prayer requests and coordinate your goals with other regional churches. It may be that your goals will change when the church planting committee begins to understand the community.

- *Form and train a church planting committee.* It is impossible to imagine a more productive church committee than this. Many committees never function properly for lack of training and specific instructions. In training them personally as pastor you are getting them off on the right foot and are proclaiming to them that you think their work is of vital importance.

- *Begin publicizing your committee's demographic findings.* Give time in your church services for a committee member to give brief reports. Begin educating your church by putting weekly statements in the bulletin of the "Did you know?" variety. Examples: Did you know that only 41 percent of our community attends church on a given Sunday? Did you know that 13,000 Chinese live within a 10-mile radius of our church and that there are only three churches to reach them for Christ? Did you know that if every person in our community decided to go to church next Sunday 78 percent of them could not find a place to sit?

• *Begin praying earnestly as a congregation about becoming a parent church.* The prayer focus should be on national, regional and local church involvement. Make an effort to sign up a significant portion of your church to become part of the worldwide family of prayer partners.

• *Let the church planting committee function and report to the board until you have in mind both the location and plan for church planting.* One of the biggest reasons good ideas fail is lack of planning. The committee needs to continue to work on its first project until everyone feels that the plan and procedure for moving forward is born of God.

• *Report your findings and intentions to the regional office of the denomination.* They must give input into the planning process. The regional denominational office will help you avoid errors and will assist in making the planting of a new church a joyful experience.

Plan dates for the initiation of the first phase of church planting. The first phase may be the beginning of a Bible study or a branch Sunday school. Whatever it is, make it an important item on your church calendar. You may want to plan a special service where plans are announced and principal persons come forward for special prayer.

CHURCH PLANTING COMMITTEE

PURPOSE

• To create a climate in the mother church that is conducive to beginning a new work.

• To identify target communities for new churches by studying the mother church and surrounding communities and establishing priorities.

- To present the facts and recommendations to the regional denominational office.

- To present the facts and recommendations to the church board.

- To work under the direction of the church board and regional office in order to implement and promote the new church-planting project.

- To nurture and assist the new church until it is organized.

FREQUENCY OF MEETINGS

The committee should meet monthly at a regularly scheduled time for reports, discussing needs and receiving feedback. Minutes of each meeting should be given to the church board and the regional office.

SELECTION OF THE CHURCH PLANTING COMMITTEE

The committee should have from three to five members, appointed by the church board.

- They should be persons who are respected by the congregation, missionary-minded, Spirit-filled and concerned about the lostness of people.

- They should be able to gather and analyze data, to work with people and be willing to work.

- Their personalities should be warm, loving, caring and optimistic. They need leadership qualifications.

TRAINING OF COMMITTEE MEMBERS

There are materials available for the pastor to train committee members adequately. Besides this manual itself, the materials listed in the resource section will be a big help in preparing and training your committee. Other materials may be available through your denominational office.

TRAINING THE CHURCH PLANTING COMMITTEE

The training of the church planting committee should be done by the pastor and regional office. The pastor and perhaps a key lay leader should be trained in church planting strategies.

A couple of two-hour training sessions should be adequate to thoroughly train the committee members. You may want to schedule a third training session four to six months later to review progress and do further teaching in the areas where they need more specific skills.

One week prior to the first two-hour session, give each committee member a copy of this manual. Instruct them to read the entire book and jot down questions that need to be answered during the two sessions.

In Session One, with your regional extension director present, take one-and-a-half hours to go over this manual section by section. Give an overview of each section so that your members will understand the theology and philosophy behind parent church planting. Emphasize each point which seems important to you and give time for your committee members to ask questions. Save the church planting committee job description for last. Except for a brief description, skip the section on demographics because it will be a major part of your second training session.

Next, take 15 minutes to go over the job description of the church planting committee, making sure that they understand the vital importance of their task. In the second session you will train them in the specifics of their job.

Take the remaining 15 minutes asking the Lord of the harvest to help you as pastor, the committee members and the church in general see the lost in your community through His eyes.

In Session Two, along with the regional director, spend the first hour training the church planting committee to do demographic work. It is important for you to understand how to do demographic studies yourself. Read some of the suggested books in the Index that will help you understand how to do demographic work. Discover the places in the subject community where data can be gathered. Do some homework yourself at these places so that you will be able to demonstrate to the committee how to gather data. Don't do the work for the committee, however, because discovering the people that your church is not reaching is an important part of the committee's training.

In the next 45 minutes go over the job description thoroughly. Spend adequate time emphasizing the spiritual and attitudinal qualities of the committee members. Give them your vision of what you would like to accomplish, i.e., five daughter churches in 10 years.

In this 45-minute period also go over schedules with them. Tell them when and where they will regularly meet and to whom they will report. Also give a layout of what you want them to accomplish in the first year. Tell them how you plan to publicize their findings and their recommendations. Be sure they understand that you are excited about the great prospect of impacting the community through their work.

Spend the remaining 15 minutes praying that the anointing of the Holy Spirit will be on them as they work to reach their community for Christ.

THE DISTRICT-INITIATED CHURCH

As we consider the hundreds and thousands of communities across the United States it becomes obvious that many do not have enough gospel-preaching churches. These population centers are in desperate need of the gospel of Jesus Christ. If church parenting is not possible, can we somehow still plant churches? How is it possible?

THE REGIONAL EXTENSION DIRECTOR

The primary responsibility of the regional extension director is to plant churches. Although there are a number of options as to how a church may be started, it remains that the director must continually be taking the initiative in thrusting out into the areas as yet untouched by the church in much the same way as an overseas missionary.

It could be a major city, a medium or even a small town which he targets. It could be the inner city or the suburbs, or a cross-cultural outreach to specific ethnic groups.

Regardless, it is incumbent upon the regional director to develop a church-planting strategy in order to reach every community in his district. The following approaches are possible ways for the director to establish contacts in a community.

Denominational Magazine

It will surprise many to find how widespread are former members of the denominational churches. Because of the mobile society in which we live, church people have scattered all across the country. Many continue to subscribe to the denominational magazine. Thus there is still a strong and vital contact with these committed people.

Christians Looking for a Church

Often a group of believers has begun meeting in a particular community with the intent of starting a new church, only to find that without the fellowship and leadership of a parent organization they flounder and eventually die. Some, to their credit, begin to search for an evangelical denomination with which to identify. Your church very often is exactly what they are looking for. However, they need first to discover you! How can this be done? Here are a few suggestions:

Christian Bookstores
- Place an attractive poster and Christian brochures in each of the local Christian bookstores. This is logical because so many believers visit bookstores.

Radio Announcements
- Place public service announcements on all the local radio stations regarding your desire to plant a new church in the area.

Newspaper Ads
- Run a series of attractive and informative ads on the church page of the local newspaper.

Para-Church Groups
- Meet with the leaders of the various para-church organizations to inform them about the new church.

No doubt there are other creative ways to make the church known in a community. All should be vigorously pursued, because there are always individual Christians and groups of Christians looking for a home. Let's give them the home they are seeking!

Independent churches sometimes grow weary of standing alone and begin to search for a denomination. They tire of trying to find competent pastors, missionaries and fellowships with which to identify. True, we must proceed with great caution due to doctrinal distinctives, theological differences and other issues of great importance to the denomination. However, there is merit in making yourselves known to independent churches.

When one hears of an independent church looking for a denomination, the regional office should be contacted for proper follow-up.

Many times an independent church has declined in size so far that they can be only an initial church group for the starting of a new church.

The Church Planter's Personal Contacts

Very often a pastor who has responded to God's call to plant a new church in a given community will have friends, family or even former church members living in the area. It is not at all unusual for these to form the initial church group.

THIRTEEN WAYS TO START A CHURCH

SENDING FORTH

We mention this first because it is the usual way of thinking about mothering a church. When you hive off a group, after you have grown to a certain size, you give people to start another church. If there are church leaders and musicians in that group, this becomes a very effective way to plant a church. In sending forth, the new church is able almost from the beginning to support a pastor.

PASTORAL STAFF TO PLANT A CHURCH

A successful extension pastor may be hired to be on the staff of a large church. His job as assistant pastor could be to plant other churches in the community and nearby communities. You may want to have your church involved in paying the salary of a staff person whose job it is to do evangelism through the planting of other churches.

START A RESURRECTION-SUNDAY CHURCH

Once you have identified a good place to begin a church through your demographic studies, use the "Resurrection Sunday." The idea here is to begin services on Easter Sunday, the Sunday when most people will attend a church. A huge publicity blitz and extensive planning are necessary for this type of start, but often you will have 200 to 300 in attendance in that first meeting! Your church would be involved in praying, addressing envelopes, forming the ministry team and paying for start-up costs. A temporary pastor may be supplied from your church staff, or you may work with the district office to find a permanent pastor. A manual explaining this program is available. Check the "Index of Helps" in the back of this manual for information.

THE PASTOR AS THE CATALYST

Starting a new church may be as simple as a pastor burdened for his community being a catalyst and initiating action. Many of us have driven across town or to the next town on our day off to hold a Bible study for the purpose of planting a church. Perhaps a pastor seeing an ethnic group which his church is not reaching will initiate action by calling the regional office or the appropriate ethnic regional office. He will commit time for leg work and prayer and continued conversations with the appropriate people until action is taken.

USING AN ELDER TO START AN EVANGELISTIC BIBLE STUDY

In even the smallest church, an elder who has a burden for the lost and the ability to teach could be used to plant a church. Having chosen the location, the elder begins evangelistic Bible studies. As people are saved, they are brought to the mother church for discipling and fellowship. They know from the beginning, however, that at a certain point a church will be started in their community using them as the ministry team. When the time comes to plant the church, the regional office will assist you in finding a pastor and in properly organizing the new church.

HOLDING SUMMER VACATION BIBLE SCHOOLS

Your church could hold a vacation Bible school in a selected location for one or even several years. If your church sponsors the Bible school, people will be more willing to send their children. By creatively using the prospect list in follow-up visitation, you may be able to find several families who would love to become a part of a new church.

STARTING A BRANCH SUNDAY SCHOOL

There are churches all over the country who started as a Sunday school. This was a common way to plant churches in the past and it is still an effective way. You could sponsor a branch Sunday school using volunteer teachers from your church. After a couple of years of faithful teaching, you would have gathered a number of people who could become the core membership of a new church.

USING DIFFERENCES IN PHILOSOPHY OF MINISTRY

With this option you have to read carefully or else you will not be able to move beyond hurt feelings to see this common sense approach to church planting. Sooner or later in any growing church, people leave the church because they do not see eye-to-eye with the pastor on one or several issues. Maybe they do not like the ministry style of the pastor or the church. It could be a simple matter of philosophy of ministry differences that is causing the unrest. To stay with the church would mean continual pain for them, and so they decide to leave. Usually these people end up in another denomination or in an independent church. Our tendency as pastors is to:

- think that if they were spiritual they would adjust to our way of thinking and stay with us;

- feel that if they leave our church we do not want them to go to any church.

Both of these attitudes are reactionary and wrong. Barring deep moral or spiritual problems, why not use them to start another church? In this way several things happen which are good:

- You have learned to use philosophy of ministry differences in a way which is glorifying to the Lord.

- Rather than having a feeling of rejection, these people will feel positive love for the pastor and congregation who loved them enough to help them plant this church.

- Your church can be involved in the excitement of mothering. A sister church will be born to help you reach the community for Christ.

APPOINT LAY PEOPLE FOR CHURCH PLANTING

As the early church set apart Paul and Barnabas, so there are probably people in your congregation with the necessary church-planting gifts who would be honored to be commissioned as church-planting missionaries. They would continue as members of your church and work under your direction.

BEGIN AN ETHNIC SUNDAY SCHOOL CLASS

After discovering a significant number of ethnic people in your community, initiate Sunday school classes in your church for this group. The adults should be taught in their own language. The children may feel comfortable in your regular English-speaking classes. When you visit these people, tell them that as soon as there is a large enough group you will help them start their own church with their own pastor.

INVITE AN ETHNIC CHURCH TO BEGIN IN YOUR FACILITY

In your demographic study you may find a large ethnic population. Language and cultural barriers will prevent them from coming to your church. Rather than trying to start a church among them on your own, invite the appropriate ethnic district to start a church using your facilities. Your part in this church-planting effort will be prayer and the free use of facilities for two or three years.

USE LONG-DISTANCE DRIVERS

The question is often asked, "How large do we have to be before we can start another church?" The answer is that any size church can start a church if it is open to opportunities. For example, you may have some very good people who are driving a long distance to your church. They want to be fully involved but find it difficult because of the distance. Even though they love your church, you find them attending less and less. Soon they will drop out altogether. Before this happens, talk over the possibility of your church mothering a church in their neighborhood using them as a core family. Use their home as a Bible study location and begin laying prayerful plans for mothering a church.

GIVE MONEY AND PRAYER SUPPORT FOR A CHURCH IN A REMOTE PART OF YOUR DISTRICT

We put this last because it is our conviction that even a rural church can start another church in a nearby town or somewhere in the county. In the unlikely event that this is impossible and you still want to be involved in helping to start a new church, you may want to call the regional office and arrange a way to sponsor a church in a remote part of your district.

SUMMARY THOUGHTS

These are just a few suggestions as to how to gather a group of Christians to form the initial church group. There are most certainly other methods and means. Suffice it to say that whether it be the parent church, district-initiated contacts, an independent group or the church planter himself who forms the church group as the beginning ministry team, there is always a way to start an exciting new church in any community.

We must not limit ourselves to simply one method! As we progress through this training manual you will discover other very helpful ways to start a successful evangelistic and growing church.

WHAT DOES IT COST TO START A CHURCH?

This is one of the most commonly asked questions. However the answer is quite simple. There is no set cost! Each new church is different. The circumstances are unique and therefore the costs vary. Here are a few cost factors to consider.

INITIAL COSTS

1. *A visit to the community* to conduct a demographic study is necessary. Transportation, housing, meals and research materials could be the earlier costs in church planting. Often a regional office of your denomination will absorb this, especially if the extension director does the survey.

2. *A visit by the church planter to the community* is necessary prior to his committal to start the new church.

3. *Advertising* to gain attention and recognition is mandatory.

4. *Initial literature* for community handouts is often used.

5. *Moving* the pastor, as well as rental deposit, utility hookups and other related costs, are important expense items to be considered.

6. *Pastoral support* is very important. Some church planters can handle

being bivocational, but most need either partial or full subsidy. Of course the length of time subsidy is needed must be weighed.

7. *Facility and equipment rental* should be carefully considered.

8. *Worship, Sunday school and other supplies* are necessary.

The church planter in conjunction with the regional office should carefully detail the projected start-up costs for the new church and establish the operating budget accordingly.

The start-up costs for a new church vary from place to place, but it is most important to thoroughly plan and project over one, two and three years the budget needed to assist the new work until it becomes self-supporting.

SELECTION OF A COMMUNITY

Whether it is the regional office, a parent church or the individual pastor desiring to plant a new church, the first consideration is how and where to select the right community. The following are a few suggestions to stimulate thinking.

A GENERAL RESEARCH OF COMMUNITIES

Conduct a general research study of the communities in your region to learn everything possible about them. Determine the economy, industries and other pertinent demographic information. Your regional U.S. Census Bureau will provide you with facts you need to know. Also the local Chamber of Commerce provides (often free of charge) sufficient information to have an adequate folder of materials on each subject community. Narrow down the number of communities to perhaps three or four.

AN ON-SITE VISIT TO THE SELECTED COMMUNITIES

Visit the Chamber of Commerce, drive throughout the community and meet the pastors, para-church leaders, Christian bookstore and radio station managers. Attempt to obtain a strong cross-sectional understanding of the community from Christian leaders.

FINAL COMMUNITY SELECTION

The above-mentioned demographic study, assisted by information from the Census Bureau and the Chamber of Commerce, will save you valuable time, energy and money. In order to arrive at a final decision on an area in the selected community you must determine the kind of people to whom you feel you can minister. With which cultural, ethnic, professional or economic grouping are you able to identify and communicate effectively? This will assist you in determining in which area of the community the church should concentrate.

TARGETING AN AREA OF THE COMMUNITY

Concentrate on the area of the community you have selected. Research it most carefully.

Schools, community centers, commercial buildings, clubs, churches, airport, recreational area, parks, apartments, condominiums, new housing developments and other residential areas must be thoroughly examined if the ideal church meeting place and future site is to be found. Please refer to the section dealing with selecting the first meeting place in order to obtain detailed suggestions.

THE COMMUNITY SURVEY

It is recommended that this be completed prior to denominational approval being granted for the continuation of this project.

Complete and Submit to Regional Office

Person making survey:_____ Date_____

I. GENERAL INFORMATION

    1. City:_____ State:_____

    2. Subdivision:_____

    3. Attach map of the city

II. DEMOGRAPHIC DATA

    1. Population: _____ City _____ Subdivision _____ County____

        a. 10 yrs. ago _____

        b. 5 yrs. ago _____

        c. 2 yrs. ago _____

    2. Projected:

        a. Next 2 yrs. _____

        b. Next 5 yrs. _____

        c. Next 10 yrs. _____

    3. Population trends:

        a. Population is: increasing ____ declining ____

        b. Area is: city ____ suburban ____ rural ____

        c. Families are: young____middle-aged____elderly____mixed____

d. Housing area is: duplex ___ single dwelling ___

apartment ___ condos ___

III. SOCIOLOGICAL DATA

1. List the primary occupations in the target area:

Firm	No. of Employees	Product
_____		
_____		
_____		
_____		
_____		

2. What major ethnic groups are in the area? _____

3. Is there evidence of change in the target neighborhood?_____

Why?_____

IV. COMMUNITY FACILITIES

1. Fire protection: _____full-time_____volunteer_____

2. Medical facilities: How many?

Hospitals_____

Nursing Homes_____

Doctors _____

Dentists _____

3. Churches: How many?

Denominational _____

Fundamental _____

Charismatic _____

Evangelical _____
(List on back side, including size, growing, static or declining.)

4. Motels: How many? _____

5. Public schools: Enrollment

   Elementary _____ _____

   Junior High _____ _____

   Senior High _____ _____

6. Colleges:

   Junior   _____ _____
   Trade &
   Vocational _____ _____

   Christian   _____ _____

   Universities _____ _____

7. Financial institutions:

   Commercial banks _____

   Savings and loans _____

8. Communications:

   Newspapers _____

   Radio stations
   Christian _____ Secular _____

   Television stations _____

   Cable _____

9. Recreation Facilities:

   Parks _____

Bowling _____

Swimming _____

Skating rink _____

Tennis courts _____

Other _____

10. Transportation:

Railroad _____

Airport _____

Bus _____

Ferry _____

Other _____

V. REAL ESTATE

1. Is a temporary meeting place available? _____

2. What and where? _____

3. Visibility? _____ Accessibility? _____ Excess Parking? _____

4. Rent or lease amount: _____

5. Property:

a. Are homes available? Purchase _____ Rent _____

b. Cost to purchase a home $_____

c. Cost to rent a home $_____

d. Is land available? $_____

e. If so, land cost per acre? $_____

6. Where is the most desirable location for a new church?

_____

VI. ECONOMIC DATA

1. Average family income: $_____

2. Property tax structure per $1,000:

   City _____

   County _____

VII. DENOMINATION DATA

1. List the nearest churches of the denomination: (Pastor, miles)

_____

_____

2. How many denominational magazine subscribers are there in the city?_____ Attach list.

3. How many people of your denomination are residing in the area who are not attending one of its churches?_____

4. List seed families: Occupation   No. of Children

(1)_____

(2)_____

(3)_____

(4)_____

(5)_____

(6)_____

(7)_____

EFFECTIVE DEMOGRAPHIC RESEARCH

DEFINITION

Webster's definition of demography is "the statistical study of human populations especially with reference to size and density, distribution and vital statistics."

OBSERVATIONS OR FACTS

Know who the people are in your community. Do not assume that you know who they are through observation. A pastor of a church in southern California observed that his community was quickly becoming ethnic. He wondered if it was possible for his church to survive. Notice that I said he observed the change. However, when he did his demographic study, he learned that his community was 70 percent Anglo and that the change was advancing very slowly.

PURPOSE OF DEMOGRAPHICS

Wrong assumptions mean that you will build faulty foundations. You need accurate, up-to-date information concerning the people surrounding your new church. The purpose of demographics is to let you know who your target groups are and how to reach them. Some pastors love to collect information, make charts and color in graphs! I know a pastor who never had a church with over 50 in attendance, yet he could assemble a masterpiece of demographic information. He could produce a beautiful book but could not grow a church! You should collect enough information so that you will know who are the unreached and understand best how to reach them. The end of demographics is a dynamic, growing church that meets people's needs.

TIME COMMITMENT

How much time will it take to do enough demographics so that you understand your area of ministry? Everything that you need to know for the initial stage of your church-planting effort can be gathered in the first couple of weeks after your arrival on the scene.

The kind of demographic information you need to gather can be easily found and falls into four categories:

1. Who are the people groups in your community?
2. How many of them are unchurched and who goes to church?
3. What are the largest and fastest growing churches doing to attract people?
4. What do the unchurched people in your community think about church?

RESULTS

When this information is gathered, you will know:

- What group or groups of people to target first.
- How many churches need to be planted in the community.

- What kind of worship, programming and outreach is needed to be successful.
- What resources need to be prayed about in order to function dynamically.
- Where the best location is to start your church.

GATHERING INFORMATION

Detailed census information is gathered every 10 years with some updating in between the decades. Complete census information broken down as small as census tracts can be found in your city or county library. Two afternoons in the library will give you most of the information you will need. The Chamber of Commerce and your city or county government offices will provide trends and the economy of the area. A third source worth mentioning is the public schools. They build their budgets on numbers of students so that accurate demographic information is very important to them.

One of the side benefits of doing this research is that it gives you the opportunity to introduce yourself to the librarian, the school superintendents and various governmental workers. Knowing them is an important part of knowing your community.

DETERMINING THE TARGET

How wide an area should you survey? That depends entirely on your vision. By examining a large area you will no doubt discover that there is a need for several churches, so you will want to develop a church that will plant other churches. You will build this thought into your plans and into the minds of your church people from the very beginning. If you are not sure who to target first or where to meet, a survey of a large area will help you identify the most fertile areas. Once you have identified the area where you will establish your church, you may want to go back to your sources to do a more microscopic look at the area closest to your church building.

There are few true neighborhood or community churches, since most people now drive to church. They will pass dozens of churches to attend one that meets their needs, and where they will be given freedom and trust to develop ministries according to their spiritual gifts and God-given abilities.

CATEGORIES

Divide your community into the following categories: ethnic or language groups, age groups, education status and economic status. Also, include special statistics such as the number of singles, divorced or one-parent families. Note special communities, such as those with colleges or universities, which may help to determine the different ministries you are going to have.

USE A MAP

It may be helpful to picture the above information on a map so that you can see different pockets of people in an area, if such is the case. Now compare your current statistics with the previous census statistics in order to see the changes in numbers and balance of people.

- Is there a significant growth in ethnic groups?

- Is there a shift in the average age of population?
- Are the economic and education bases changing?

This will give you accurate up-to-date information about your community and help you keep from making plans based on false assumptions.

HOW MANY ARE UNCHURCHED? WHO GOES TO CHURCH?

After your basic demographic information is gathered, it is time to find out the percentage of unchurched people and who they are. Of course, it is impossible to get totally accurate information on this, because you are not going to do a personal interview with each person in your target area. An additional factor is that no one has a precise definition on what constitutes the unchurched. You and I would say that a person who attends church on Christmas and Easter is unchurched, but others might argue the point. For your purposes, you are going to find out the average morning worship attendance of all the congregations in your area, whether Catholic, Protestant, Jewish or cults, and subtract that number from the number of people that live in the community. This will give you an approximate percentage of unchurched people who will become your target group. (The national average ranges between 60 to 80 percent unchurched.)

How do you do this? Very simple! Call or visit each pastor or his secretary and ask them. If you make a friendly personal visit, you will be killing two birds with one stone: gathering statistics and building bridges with community people.

Warning: Validate with research what some pastors, especially of the smaller churches, will tell you about the community. I know of many church-planting pastors who believed the other pastors who said that the community was impossible to reach for Christ. Armed with that attitude, these men failed. What else could happen? *Your attitude is everything!*

Some of these men, if they discern that you are on the ball, will be threatened by your arrival. They will tell you that there are already too many churches in the community. This is false. There are not too many churches until the entire community is reached. Your study will reveal a large percentage of unchurched. You will be able to discern both the percentage and number of people who are not going to church.

These pastors may also tell you how hard people are to reach for Christ. This is also wrong. You should believe Jesus who said, "The harvest is plentiful," rather than those pastors with negative attitudes. There are scores of pastors who could go into any community, including yours, and start a thriving church because they possess leadership, drive, faith and a burden for the lost. They know how to be up-to-date and relevant and are reaching people. You should be one of them.

Here is an example of what you might say, either over the phone or in person: "Hello, I'm Bill Jones, pastor of the new _____ church. We are trying our best to build our church by targeting those who do not go to church. To help us get a handle on the numbers we are talking about, I am calling on all the pastors to find out how many people in our community attend church on an average Sunday. Would you please tell me your average morning worship attendance?"

At the same time you are talking to pastors about their worship attendance, you should ask them to give their best estimate of the average age of their church. Your list might begin something like this:

CHURCH	WORSHIP ATTENDANCE	AVERAGE AGE
Community Baptist	125	50
Assemblies of God	400	40
Nazarene	85	65
Our Lady, Roman Catholic	1,075	55
Christ Revival Center	1,500	35
Methodist	250	60
First Alliance	275	50

Knowing the approximate age group of each church will tell you two things: first, the pockets of people by age that are not being reached by the churches in the community; and second, what age groups are attracted to the most successful churches. I have noticed that a live, contemporary worship style attracts young couples who otherwise would have dropped out of church. But that same contemporary style attracts people of every age.

WHAT ARE THE LARGEST AND FASTEST GROWING CHURCHES DOING TO ATTRACT PEOPLE?

VISIT GROWING CHURCHES

The next demographic work you need to do is to find out what the largest and fastest growing churches are doing to attract people. To find this out, first, you should attend the largest and fastest growing churches and observe what goes on there.

Most people do not attend church because they have done a detailed study of a church's doctrinal statement. This may be true of a few, but very few. Church growth experts agree that denominational loyalty which keeps people going to one kind of church is almost a thing of the past. Today, people will go to a church that meets their felt needs or they will not go at all. If you provide a caring, relevant church, people will come.

Your main assignment in going to the services of the larger churches in town is to put together a list of qualities that stand out in those churches.

- How would you describe the leadership of the pastor?
- What is the worship service like?
- Did the church seem caring?
- Was it well organized?
- What special features jump out at you as you sit in the service?

The second thing you should do is ask a few people casually why they come to this church. Say, "I'm Bill Jones, and I'm new in town. I visited today because your church is one of the largest in town. Why do you think people are attracted to this church?"

Third, make an appointment for lunch with the pastor. You pay the bill, of course! Tell him who you are and exactly why you are in town. Tell him you attended his church because you wanted to find out what attracted people to his church. Ask him what he thinks the ingredients are to his successful church. Then say something like, "I'm pretty new at this and would love to be as successful as you in reaching people for Christ. If you were me, what are some of the main things you would do to develop a dynamic church?"

A pastor of a large church will not be intimidated by your presence. Not only does he feel secure in his large church, but usually a man who can grow a large church is not jealous of other leaders. He may even feel paternal toward you and be glad you came to him for help. A humble but sincere attitude on your part toward the more successful pastors in your community may yield not only useful information but other benefits such as musicians on loan from their church to help you as you begin planting your church.

WHAT DO THE UNCHURCHED PEOPLE IN YOUR COMMUNITY THINK ABOUT CHURCH?

ASK THEM!

The last part of your demographic study is to find out what the unsaved and unchurched think about church. Why aren't they attending? What are their felt needs that you should address in your new church? Whenever a new church starts, the primary target is the unsaved and the unchurched. Major strategies will be centered around attracting those who need the Lord. Therefore, it is important to know what they are thinking. How do you know what they think? You *ask* them!

We recommend the "Resurrection Sunday Manual," originated by Southern Baptist pastor Rick Warren. His church in the Saddleback community of southern California started with 200 people on the first Sunday and has grown to thousands. We can expect the same results if we do our homework and show strong visionary leadership. See the "Index of Helps" for further information on this manual.

Accurate information can help you minimize your mistakes and plan a church which will be attractive to people and glorifying to the Lord. What you find out may challenge your thinking about how things should be done. One of the saddest and most tragic indictments on the church is that so many pastors and lay leaders seem to be saying, "If people want to accept Christ, they can do it our way, or we won't reach them at all!"

Be flexible. The apostle Paul said, "I have become all things to all men so that by all possible means I might save some" (1 Corinthians 9:22).

GOD'S CLEAR DIRECTION

Commit every step of your decision-making process to God in prayer. Ask Him to open the door of opportunity and give you clear direction in the selection of your community and area for the planting of an exciting new church!

FORMATION STEPS FOR A NEW CHURCH

The following is a simple overview of the various steps in planting a new church. You will notice the left column is the various stages and the right column represents those individuals and/or groups responsible for the corresponding stages.

STEPS	RESPONSIBLE LEADERS

Beginning Stage

Interested families contacted
Church group established
Denominational doctrines and distinctives
    examined
Commitments made by interested families
Local bank account opened
Church name selected

> Regional Extension Director
> Church Planter

Formative Stage

Adoption of a provisional constitution
Appointment of advisory committee
Appointment of pastor
Arrangement for meeting place
Announcement to community

> Regional Extension Director
> Church Planter
> Advisory Committee

Church Organized/Incorporated

Adoption of denomination's church
    constitution
Adoption of articles of incorporation
Election of church officers/church board
Formation of charter membership
Local church bylaws developed and adopted

> Pastor
> Congregation
> Church Board
> District Leadership

Church Relationship

Member church of denomination
Full representation to annual council of the denomination in North America
All privileges and responsibilities of the denomination manual become operative for the local church.
All privileges and responsibilities of the regional denominational bylaws become operative for the local church.

CHECK LIST FOR THE NEW CHURCH

When you assume the responsibility of planting a new church there are numerous details which you must care for. This is a check list that will help you through the early days and months. It is not comprehensive and you may wish to add a number of other items. Post this by your desk so you can refer to it on a daily basis. The order of items may be adjusted to conform to the local situation.

ITEM	NOT APPLICABLE	IN PROCESS	DATE ACCOMPLISHED
Select Community			
Community Demographics			
Pastor Appointed			
Pastoral Orientation to Community			
Recruit Ministry Team			
Wall Planning Calendar for Pastor			
Interested Persons Meeting			
Church Name Chosen			
Local Bank Account Opened			
Treasurer & Assistant Chosen			
Subsidy Scale Established			
Advisory Committee Appointed			
Budget Established			
Obtain Post Office Box or Mailing Address			
Select Meeting Place			
Purchase Liability Insurance			
File Nonprofit Corporation Papers			
Apply for Bulk Mailing Permit			
Acquire Equipment/Supplies (list)			
Plan in detail first 4 Worship Services (list)			
Train Ministry Team (See following list)			
Worship Leader			
Instrumentalists			
Song Leaders			
Soloists			
Group Singers			
Sound Technician			
Head Usher			
Ushers (4)			
Sound and Tapes Technician			
Greeters			

Children's Ministries Director   _____

     Nursery Workers   _____
     Toddler Workers   _____
     Children's Church Leaders   _____
     Sunday School Teachers (all ages)   _____

Teen Ministries Director   _____
College Ministries Director
(Singles and/or college)   _____
Young Professionals Director   _____
Mid-Adults Director   _____
Senior Adults Director   _____

Special Events Director   _____
Decorations   _____

Social Events Coordinator   _____
     Receptions/Showers Coordinator   _____

Recruitment Secretary (Volunteer)   _____

     Office Workers   _____

Evangelism Ministries Coordinator   _____

     Friendship Evangelism   _____
     Evangelism Explosion   _____
     Radio Program   _____
     Direct Mailings   _____
     Telephone Outreach   _____
     Other   _____

Professionally Done Signs
     (Exterior/Interior)   _____
Professionally Designed Stationery   _____
Bulletins, Registration Cards, etc.   _____
Advertising & Publicity Director   _____
Train Membership Class Teachers   _____
Missionary Conference Chairperson   _____
Communicating Missions Manuals Ordered _____
Plan Worship Services 4-6 Months in Advance _____
Plan Yearlong Strategy for Church
(Use the wall calendar for specific plans) _____
     One-month Goal   _____
     Three-month Goal   _____

Six-month Goal   _____

One-year Goal   _____

Two-year Goal   _____

Women's President   _____

Men's President   _____

POTENTIAL NEW CHURCH SURVEY FORM

We are excited about planting a new church in our community! In order to do so we must gather some preliminary information from interested people. Please complete this questionnaire and return it to the regional office at your earliest convenience.

PLEASE TYPE OR PRINT

Date_____

Community _____ State _____

Your Name _____ Phone (___)_____

Address _____

       Street   City   State   Zip

Names of persons interested in starting a new church:

_____   _____

_____   _____

_____   _____

How many adults are from the denomination's background? _____

Are you now meeting together? _____ Bible study?_____ Prayer?____

Would you like to have a Bible study? _____

Would you like to either host or teach a study? _____

What total could be expected from the group in monthly tithes and offerings?

$_____

(necessary information)

What is the population of your community? _____ County_____

How many evangelical churches are in your town? _____

Why would you like to have a new church? _____

By what date would you like to have a new church started?_____

Do you have a particular pastor in mind? _____

The regional extension director would like to visit and conduct an "interested persons meeting." If so, what date and time would be convenient for you and other interested persons? _____

PLEASE NOTE OTHER INFORMATION ON THE BACK
OF THIS QUESTIONNAIRE.

THE INTERESTED PERSONS MEETING

The purpose of conducting an interested persons meeting is to lay the proper foundation for the planting of a new church. The meeting should be conducted by the regional office leadership. If the church planting pastor has already been appointed then he will be present but not chair the meeting.

(1) Accountability

Regardless of how the new work is being started, whether by a parent-church congregation or an independent group interested in joining the denomination, the regional extension director or his representative is responsible for meeting with the initial group in order to give direction as to proper procedures, accountability and other pertinent information.

All decisions regarding the establishment of a new church must be cleared through the regional office. If a parent church is initiating the church start, the senior pastor and his board must first meet with the regional extension director to establish the proper guidelines.

(2) Invitations, Advertising, Publicity

Following the suggestions noted in the previous section, "Forming the Initial Core Group" (page 21), the regional director or his key contact people will make a concerted effort to gather a group of Christians who have expressed interest in starting a new church.

(3) Proper Location and the Host Family

If the expected attendance is less than 15 adults it is recommended that a home be selected for a meeting place in order to create an informal atmosphere. Great care must be given to this choice. The chairman should visit the suggested homes to see if the meeting area is appropriate. He should take note of:

- *The neighborhood*
  Does it represent an average area in which the invited people would feel comfortable or would they have difficulty identifying with the location and environment?

- *The house*
  Note the overall appearance.

  Is it neat and well-maintained?

  Is it clean and nicely decorated?

  Is it easy to locate?

- *The meeting area*

  This could be the living room or family room.

  Is it well lighted and comfortable?

  Do they have enough seating?

- *Distractions*

  There should be no pets in the house. Many people have allergies, and this would be a serious barrier.

  The TV, radio or stereo should be turned off.

  If the invited people have small children, arrangements should be made to care for them—either in a separate part of the host home or in a nearby home.

- *The Host Family*

  Do they represent a good cross-section of the people who have been invited?

  Are they truly committed to starting the new church? Are they enthusiastic?

(4) Agenda

The regional extension director or his representative should meet with the host family prior to the meeting in order to brief and prepare them for the meeting. The agenda should be discussed so that they will know what to expect. Simple refreshments should be planned for after the meeting, keeping in mind that children may be present. The meeting should not exceed an hour and 45 minutes with a 30-minute fellowship following.

The following is a suggested agenda for the Interested Persons Meeting:

7:00 Extension director arrives with the church planter. Briefing with host family and time of prayer.

7:30 Arrival of invited interested persons. Devotional and prayer—focusing on church planting as New Testament evangelism.

7:45 Presentation of video and literature on the denomination.

8:00 Presentation of regional church planting guidelines/policies by extension director.

8:15 Illustration of recent successful church beginnings.

8:30 Challenge to those present regarding the starting of the new church.

8:45 Challenge to a financial commitment by those present. (You need to know what to expect financially on a monthly basis in order to establish a pastoral and operational support base.) No one is obligated.

- Pass out blank slips of paper for people to jot down their preliminary commitment. Ask someone to tally up the amounts without giving any names.

- Announce the total monthly amount. Give thanks to God. Select a treasurer and a local bank.

9:00 Discuss initial meetings. A home Bible study, a fellowship or social meeting to get acquainted or perhaps a first public worship service will be expected by the new church group.

9:15 Dismiss with prayer. Refreshments and fellowship.

(5) Necessary Decisions and Commitments

The extension director must have with him a list of items to be covered with the new church group. Here are some suggestions:

- A video presentation on the denomination
- Denominational literature
- Regional office literature
- Denominational manual
- Regional office bylaws
- Regional office procedures for appointing a church planter
- Regional office financial/subsidy policies
- Reporting forms and procedures
- How to select a church treasurer and assistant treasurer
- How to select a local bank
- How to use the district tax-exempt number
- How to select an appropriate meeting place
- Regional office and denominational policies and regulations regarding:

  - Annual missionary conference pledges
  - Regional conference
  - Regional pastors' retreat
  - General Council of the denomination
  - Retirement fund
  - Reporting procedures
  - Giving to regional office
  - Giving to regional church planting

- Regional office policies regarding the appointment of the Advisory Committee
- Adoption of the provisional constitution for developing churches
- Official organization information
- Nonprofit incorporation information
- Nonprofit bulk-mailing permit information
- Copy of this manual

(6) A Larger Location

If a larger group is expected or if there is no acceptable host home, the extension director or the church planter should select an alternate location, such as a motel conference room or another attractive facility.

- It should be convenient to the invited people.
- The room setup should be casual, and refreshments should be provided.
- A key family should host the meeting.

EARLY FORMATION STAGES AND PROJECTS

NAMING THE NEW CHURCH

When the regional extension director meets initially with the church group and forms the extension Bible study, he will then name the church for the purpose of opening a local bank account. The church may be named after the community in which it is located. Example:

TOPEKA COMMUNITY CHURCH
of
the (denomination)

EXTENSION BIBLE STUDY

The extension Bible study should not be reported as an extension church until they begin to have Sunday worship services. The group is called an extension Bible study because they have a commitment to form a new church. The regional extension director will appoint a leader for the study group. They must not select a leader without his written approval. This is to protect the group and to keep its goal of becoming a denominational church very clear and defined.

THE CHURCH GROUP

A critical element of planting a new church is the people of the core group. They will provide a major portion of the prayer and financial support for the pastor, as well as needed leadership for the new church. We will be using the term "church group" rather than "core group." Church group is a definitive term which designates a group of Christians who meet regularly for worship, Bible study and prayer but may not as yet have a pastor or official organization recognition as a viable, cohesive unit.

The church group may have the basic structure of a church, such as the advisory committee.

THE ADVISORY COMMITTEE

It may consist of a church treasurer, an assistant treasurer, a recording secretary, a chairman, a Bible study leader, a children's ministries leader and a youth ministries leader.

Some of the church group will probably hold two or more offices temporarily. All appointments are for the length of term designated by the district office. Officers must sign the application for membership in the denomination, although there may be no actual membership until the official organization of the church.

A provisional government may be established using the Regulations for Developing Churches which is included in this manual.

The regional denominational leadership will appoint a pastor with input from the advisory committee. Normally, prior to official organization, a pastor, technically speaking, is appointed by the regional office. However, the input of the advisory committee is of utmost importance.

FORMING THE ADVISORY COMMITTEE

The advisory committee is appointed by the regional extension director. They do not have the power to vote because there is no actual membership as yet. They are to act simply as advisors to the pastor and the regional extension director. They are not a decision-making body. All decisions are to be channeled through the regional extension director. He gives the pastor the authority to act. This is to protect the new group and its identity with the denomination. Major decisions such as the name of the church, the calling of the church-planting pastor, the opening of a bank account, procedures for starting meetings, appointment of the advisory committee and major financial expenditures need to be made. These and other important items which will affect the start and the future of the church must be channeled through the regional extension director, since the new church will be under district administration until it is officially organized.

The Advisory Committee will assist the pastor in developing the various ministries of the new church. Since there is no actual membership until official organization there can be no election. Thus, all committee members must be appointed by the regional extension director. They are not a church board but a committee designed to assist the pastor in an advisory capacity. The regional office may designate the period of time the Advisory Committee will serve. Some committees will serve six months, others one year or longer.

APPOINTMENT OF TREASURER AND ASSISTANT TREASURER

The regional extension director will appoint the treasurer and assistant treasurer from two different family groups. They do not make spending decisions but have the responsibility of collecting, recording and depositing all monies. They are responsible for paying the bills and writing the regular support check for the pastor.

It is not their responsibility to set the pastor's salary or to determine when and how he should be paid. They have been appointed as custodians of the Lord's money and act on the authority given by the regional extension director. A sample financial form is provided in the manual. Permission to pay rent, utilities, allowances, insurance and pastor's support is a regular monthly or weekly responsibility once amounts have been established.

The pastor is granted authority to spend money for outreach and necessary church supplies and materials. However, he will regularly communicate with the regional extension director to be certain that all expenditures are approved. All special needs will be channeled through the regional office. This directive is to protect the new church and to be certain the denomination's distinctives and procedures are followed. Once the church is officially organized by the regional office the church will then have control of money-spending decisions.

ESTABLISHING THE PRELIMINARY FINANCIAL SYSTEM

It is important that procedures be financially proper from the start. This is more than merely a temporal matter; it is spiritual.

Financial Responsibilities to the Denomination

From the first meeting the new church must participate in and accept its responsibility as a vital part of the parent denomination. The benefits of being a member church are many. Here are a few:

- The constitution, which is the same for every church, is a valuable protector. It prevents a splinter group (which may have adopted a doctrinal position contrary to the denomination) from taking over the church.
- The regional leadership is readily available for counsel and help.
- The regional extension director, an expert in church planting and church growth, is also a constant help to the new church.
- Regional conferences, an excellent time of fellowship and equipping for pastor and lay leaders, is subsidized by the churches.
- The annual workers' retreat for pastors is a major help to the pastor, thus enhancing his ministry in the church.
- Christian education helps and training are often provided by the regional office.
- The regional camping program is greatly enhanced by cooperative efforts.
- Of course, the calling of a new pastor or assistance is made possible by the expert help of the regional office leaders.

These and many more benefits come as a result of the church's participating in the financial support of the regional office. Thus, from the beginning, as a result of the vote of all the elected delegates at the annual regional conference, each church gives to the regional office budget.

District Extension

Churches should also give to regional church planting. In some churches it is a part of the regular regional office budget. In still others the church people make an annual pledge to regional extension.

Overseas Missions

As the people give to overseas missions the moneys must be sent in each month. Do not allow funds to accumulate. Above all, never use mission moneys or any other designated gifts for other than that for which it was designated. Not only is it illegal, it is also an improper use of the Lord's money. Be sure to clearly note on the check the purpose of the gift.

Savings Account

It is strongly recommended that from the very first month of operation the new church open two savings accounts. One for a building fund and the other to send the pastor to district conferences, workers retreats and the denomination's annual meeting. A special once-per-year church growth seminar is also strongly recommended for the pastor.

Training the Treasurer

The treasurer should be thoroughly trained by the pastor and the extension director in order to follow procedures compatible with the regional and national requirements.

Selection of a Local Bank

The regional extension director will, in conjunction with the church group, select a local bank. The appointed treasurer, assistant treasurer and the pastor will have their names on the signature cards. In addition, the regional treasurer and extension director will have their names on the signature cards so the regional office tax-exempt number may be used until the local church is registered as a nonprofit, tax-exempt corporation. Laws may vary from state to state.

THE FIRST AND CONTINUING WORSHIP SERVICES

PLANNING THE FIRST WORSHIP SERVICE

Your public worship service will be the only thing a visitor will see or know about your new church, so it must be excellent in every way. The old saying "First impressions are lasting impressions" is very true. You must give yourself to thorough planning and detailed preparation. Write out a number of worship formats. Then in great detail write out every possible aspect of the various worship service ideas.

1. *Set the date* of the first public worship service. Use good judgment and planning as you examine the calendar. Avoid three-day weekends or other major events which would perhaps prevent people from attending. Easter is considered the best possible Sunday to begin worship services. The "Resurrection Sunday Manual" is a revision of the 1987 Easter 100 program, which resulted in the establishment of 101 new congregations in one day.

Further information on how to obtain this manual is available in the "Index of Helps."

2. *Select the best possible meeting place* which is likely to be accepted by the community. (See "Formation Procedures" in Chapter 3.)

3. *Deliver what is advertised.* If you have advertised a contemporary or traditional worship service, then the services must reflect that style. Therefore, before you go public you must have a very clear model and idea in mind.

4. *Borrow outstanding musicians* from growing churches in the area. Make an appointment with the senior pastor to gain his personal approval prior to discussing the idea with any member of his church. Be sure you know exactly what kind of music you want and try to hear the individual or group prior to inviting them. Always be prepared to give them either a love offering or an honorarium. Since you are a new church they will understand your financial situation. Plan to borrow music from a number of churches for the first dozen or so worship services.

5. *Lack of leaders.* A new church may start with but a few committed families or, in some cases, a group as large as 60 or 70 people. The church planter must be prepared to begin with a rather small group and thus have a shortage of capable leaders.

   Should there not be an individual capable of assisting in the worship service as a song leader, perhaps another church, or even a para-church organization will assist you at least the first few Sundays. Take the initiative and ask for help!

6. *Rehearse each worship service* with all participants, including greeters and ushers. In other words, go over the entire format on a Friday or Saturday in order to insure smoothness on Sunday morning.

7. *Rehearse your messages thoroughly.* Determine that in the power of God's Holy Spirit you are going to be the very best preacher in town. This must be done not out of pride or selfish ambition but to the praise and glory of God!

   Practice preaching the message at least five times prior to Sunday morning. It must not sound stilted, artificial or be read, but it should be delivered with a spontaneity that is from God.

   It is recommended that one begin with the book of Acts and stay with it for a lengthy period. After all, it gives the birth of the Church and your people can identify with its great stories.

   Remember, start positive, be positive, stay positive and be determined to help people who are hurting.

8. *Have a professional person design* attractive, church-personalized bulletins, offering envelopes, visitor and prayer cards, stationery and business cards.

Be consistent in the design, using a high quality paper stock. Never allow a poorly typed and reproduced bulletin or letter to be used. Maintain excellence!

9. *Pray!* Ask your church group leaders to meet with you early every morning for prayer. Pray specifically, and God will bring you the people and conversions!

10. *The baby nursery, toddler class and junior church* are critically important. Quality equipment and happy, well-trained people will be one of the most important services your church can provide.

11. *Dress code.* Beginning with the pastor, all participants must dress appropriately to meet the public. As pastor, you must set the standard and be certain all your leaders and helpers are in agreement. Again, this has to do with "first and lasting impressions."

12. *A good sound system* is far more important than we often realize. Many believe because the church may be small that a sound system is not needed. However, due to outside noise, infants and children and other factors, it is important!

13. *Have signs prepared only by professionals!* It is very common for a person in the church to offer his or her skills. Just be sure the person is a professional. You will need portable signs for the street, which must be large enough to be read from a car going by at 50 miles per hour. The signs should be in place the day before the service. They need only three things written on them: the name of the church, the time of the worship service (not the Sunday school) and the phone number.

    Most new churches are using temporary facilities, so portable, professionally designed direction signs are a must. For example: worship area, nursery, children's church, rest room, refreshments.

14. Getting through the first service. Make sure all aspects of the first service are in readiness:

    Worship service preparation:
    • Ministry team must be thoroughly trained.
    • Words to the worship songs must appear in the bulletin or on an overhead projector if no songbooks are available. Make sure that you have the appropriate copyright permissions to do this. Many churches continually break the law in this area.
    • Pastor and ministry team must be careful to speak in language that relates to the unchurched.
    • Music must be uplifting, contemporary and worshipful.

- Be conscious of time—the service should move quickly from one aspect to the next.
- All aspects of the service should be positive and encouraging.
- Keep announcements to a minimum.
- Scripture should be read and preached from a modern version of the Bible.
- Give invitation by registration or response card during the service.
- The sermon must emphasize life applications.
- Do not single out individuals, but concentrate on making everyone feel comfortable and welcome.

Facility preparation:
- First impressions are important.
- Greenery and flowers communicate a positive message.
- Room should be well lit.
- Maintain the right temperature.
- The sound system should be adequate to ensure that everyone can hear clearly.
- Consider a tape deck for background music prior to and after the service.
- Ministry team should wear name tags every Sunday.
- The literature table should have available copies of the denominational magazine and other information.
- The refreshment table should be placed in an area that is conducive to informal conversation (provide simple, finger refreshments).

Nursery preparation:
- Be sure the nursery room is large enough, bright and readily accessible.
- Provide roll-away carpet if the room is not carpeted, a minimum of three quality cribs and change table, new toys, disposable diapers, registration and name tags for the children.
- Recruit/hire nursery attendants with appropriate skills.

Children's church preparation:
- Prepare an atmosphere conducive to children's interests with posters, small tables and chairs.
- Provide registration and name tags for the children.
- Select and train teachers who work well with children.
- Use quality curriculum.

Greeters' preparation:
- Greeters should be placed in key locations such as parking lots, door-ways, hallways and other areas where necessary.
- Greeters need to be friendly and informed.

Sign location:
- Outside signs should be in place the day before the service, giving clear directions to parking and the meeting room.
- Inside signs need to clearly identify nursery, meeting room, children's rooms, restrooms and the free literature table.
- Signs should reflect the quality of excellence.

RESPONSE CARDS

It is extremely important to have some kind of response mechanism for your attenders. A sample is provided on the following page. You may copy it as is or revise to suit your needs.

INDIVIDUAL RESPONSE FORM
Confidential

Your response will be given directly to the pastor after the service. Please fold and place in the offering plate today.

Check appropriate age grouping.
☐ 0–12   ☐ 13–18
☐ 19–25   ☐ 26–35
Complete this section prior to the message.   ☐ 36–50   ☐ 51+

Name _____

Address _____
　　　　　　Street　　　　　　City/State　　　　　　Zip

Phone (   ) _____

☐ 1st-time visitor　　☐ Regular attender　　☐ Member

How I heard about the church: _____

MY PERSONAL RESPONSE
Confidential

Complete this section after the message. Fold and place in offering plate or give to the pastor.

☐ I received Christ as my Lord and Savior today.

☐ As a born-again Christian I recommitted my life to Christ today.

☐ I would like to privately discuss one of the above with a church leader.

☐ I have a special need and would like a private consultation.

☐ Will you pray for the following need? _____

_____

Special Prayer Request:　　☐ Confidential for Pastor only
　　　　　　　　　　　　☐ For church to pray

THE MEETING PLACE

When planning for the Sunday services, it is very important to select the best possible meeting place. Schools, community centers, public halls, conference rooms and attractive theaters are recommended. Try to avoid using storefronts, private homes, mortuaries and facilities that are a bit run-down. Use good judgment as to what part of town you should meet in. Try to stay as close to the region in which you wish to minister as possible. Avoid commercial areas consisting of warehouses, factories and other places that would tend to keep people from coming. Consider the kind of people you expect to reach and locate accordingly. Secure the most attractive place possible. It will be money well spent. Before securing a location, check with the regional extension director for advice and gain his permission. Here are a few thoughts and suggestions:

THE QUALITY MEETING PLACE

- Quality is often more an issue of attitude than finance.
- The mind-set to do all your work in a quality way is a statement about the God you serve.
- Look first for the ideal building and location.
- Trust the Lord to provide the place you need rather than a place you can afford.
- Once secured, redecorate the exterior and interior, giving it the appearance of permanence and ownership. Avoid the term "temporary." Rather, focus on long-term goals and objectives.

LOCATION

Visibility - Every attempt should be made to locate a facility which is easily seen by the greatest possible number of people. Main thoroughfares and popular community gathering places are recommended. Near a major freeway entrance/exit is desirable if the area is nice.

Appearance - An attractive facility will go far in appealing to new people. It must be visually appealing inside and out.

Accessibility - Can people easily get into the church parking lot? If it is difficult, fewer will come.

Parking space - Excess parking is a must. Many businesses close because the customers cannot park. This is very important!

Balance of ministry space - Does the facility provide ample rooms for nursery,

Sunday school classrooms, pastor's study, storage and, of course, an attractive room for worship?

Attitude about building in community - Use good judgment in your selection. Do not use a mortuary or an old church building with a poor reputation.

Enough room to grow - Check your growth goal. Carefully analyze every part of the ministry you expect to see developed, so you will not have to relocate soon.

OTHER CONSIDERATIONS

- Is it clean?
- Is it bright and cheery?
- Does it have equipment, chairs and tables?
- Does it have adequate heat/air conditioning? What kind? Is it noisy? What will utilities cost? Check the previous winter's bills. Do not go on someone's opinion.

TOUCHES YOU CAN ADD

- New paint
- Flowers or plants (for the front)
- Banners which can be quickly and easily hung
- Taped music
- Chairs neatly set up
- First-class bulletins and other printed matter
- Quality hymnals or overheads/slides
- Quality nursery equipment - redecorate the room
- Redecorate restrooms

RENTING OPTIONS

- School facilities
- Community buildings
- Restaurants
- Churches
- Office warehouses
- Shopping centers
- Hotel/motel
- Theater

SETTING UP THE CHURCH OFFICE —ADMINISTRATION

This is greatly neglected by some pastors and overplayed by others. Suffice it to say, a proper administrative office procedure can save the active church planter a great deal of time and energy.

THE HOME OFFICE IS NOT RECOMMENDED

The new church rarely has its own facility, thus the pastor sets up an office in his home. For some this is perfectly acceptable. However, in the majority of cases it is not adequate for a number of reasons:

- Newcomers to the church, as well as regular attenders, often do not feel comfortable coming to a private home for appointments or counseling.
- Often the home environment affords a variety of family interruptions, which individually seem acceptable, but would not occur if the office were located elsewhere.
- A regular office work schedule is most difficult to establish in the home environment.
- Recruiting volunteer secretaries to come to a home office is usually difficult and can even create awkward situations.
- The home office does not provide a source of permanence which is essential in developing the new church. The appearance of being "temporary" can damage the development of the church.

FINDING OFFICE SPACE

We recommend that the new church attempt to locate a suite of offices as close as possible to the first meeting site of the congregation. This is, of course, assuming that the church has the goal of relocating in the general area when they build or purchase their permanent facility.

1. Carefully research the various real estate management companies to find one with a good reputation in the community. Be certain you find an agent who specializes in renting and leasing retail office space. Remember, by law the realtor always represents the owner, not your church.

2. Write out in detail what you need for office location, accessibility, excess parking and floor-space layout. Know exactly your maximum allowable financial outlay, including utilities.

Use a map — Using a street map, mark with a highlighter the absolute distance boundaries you are willing to travel to an office location.

Be specific — Be very specific as to the kind of area in which you will locate. Do you desire a neighborhood setting, light industrial, shopping center, condominium or apartment which has been converted to office space?

Emphasize accessibility — Is it accessible? People should be able to find it easily.

Require excess parking — Is there adequate parking? If there is a problem in finding easy parking, it will discourage some people from coming to the office. Make things convenient!

Determine your budget — How much can the church afford? Be willing to stretch your faith and lease or rent the most attractive office suite possible. If it is shabby, it is a reflection on the ministry of your church. Check out the cost of utilities and telephone, also.

Know your space needs — How much floor space do you need? You need a private study for the pastor, a secretarial and reception room as minimum requirements. It is strongly recommended that you secure a third room to be used for meetings, office equipment and storage of church supplies.

Professional signs — Be sure to use the office building marquee to publicize your church. Also, have a professionally designed sign placed on each door. Give your new office a good professional appearance.

OFFICE FURNISHINGS

In our society it is important to maintain an attractive professional appearance. Americans have become accustomed to nice-looking offices as they visit their doctor, banker, etc. Shabby, worn-out furniture and equipment should not be used.

Nice furniture — Purchase or lease modern desks, chairs, file cabinets and reception-area furniture. Usually these are expensive items, but with careful shopping at wholesale furniture outlets or at used office equipment stores, bargains can be located. Exercise good taste in selecting your furniture. Use matched sets rather than mixing styles. If lamps are used, be sure they fit the decor. Also select pictures carefully.

The right equipment — Become informed on computers, so the equipment will suit future needs. Consult computer experts. Beware of salesmen who want to sell you out-dated equipment. Electronic typewriters should be compatible with your computer printer. Do not sacrifice quality.

Consult experts — As you add equipment always consult experts in the field. Avoid buying used, worn-out equipment. Good equipment can enhance your ministry in a multitude of ways, save you hundreds of man-hours and set you and your growing office staff free to deal with people's needs.

OFFICE STAFF

Paid secretary — It is often said that the first paid professional should be an executive secretary. To this I wholeheartedly agree. It is a puzzle to me why an active church planter would fail to immediately recruit a volunteer secretary, followed by a salaried position.

Volunteer secretary — Immediately recruit a volunteer secretary for a few hours a day, or a full day. It is recommended that the secretary be a woman whose children are grown, thus setting her free to devote herself to secretarial ministries. It is not wise to use a younger woman. In addition, a more mature woman has the wisdom and experience of years. She is able to give a word of counsel and pray with people who come to the office seeking help when the pastor is not available.

- *Computer literate* — The secretary should be computer literate, although this is not critical. She should be a good typist and organizer.
- *Good appearance* — She should dress tastefully and present a smiling, happy image to the public.
- *Pleasant personality* — The way she answers the phone, takes messages and deals with people is of incredible importance. Pleasant is the key word. Even over the phone people ought to be able to "sense" her smile!

Job description — The pastor should detail the secretary's job description, vacation and other qualifications and requirements prior to the job interview. She should not accept any projects other than those approved by the pastor.

It is recommended that the church continue to add office staff regularly, as the church grows, but maintain one secretary to assist the pastor in his multitude of responsibilities. The more he is set free from administrative concern the more effective he will be in ministry.

SAMPLE ADMINISTRATIVE PLAN FOR A CHURCH

THE PASTOR'S PART-TIME SECRETARY

The pastor's secretary is hired by the pastor with the approval of the church board. The secretary may be a contract employee of the church and will be paid on an hourly basis from the General Fund of the church. Be certain to check the correct IRS regulations on this subject.

1. The secretary shall be responsible solely to the pastor in so far as the assignment of all jobs and the job description.

2. The secretary is expected to maintain absolute confidentiality with regard to counseling, material and office assignments in general. Violation of this standard may result in the immediate dismissal of the secretary by the pastor.

3. The secretary is expected to order all necessary office supplies as needed, maintain the office checking account and prepare a quarterly report for the church board.

4. The secretary can be released from employment by the pastor without consultation with the church board. Documentation of just cause should be provided by the pastor if required.

5. The secretary is allowed two weeks vacation per year, and all official national holidays off without pay if she is a contract employee without benefits, until she is hired on a full-time basis. Holidays will not be made up by additional working hours. (Again, check with the correct IRS regulations.)

6. The secretary's working hours are 9:00 a.m. to 1:00 p.m., Monday through Friday, at a flat hourly pay rate without benefits in that she is a contract employee. The hourly pay is established by the church board and is reviewed in December each year, along with all other contract employees.

7. The secretary may be allowed special time off if a qualified substitute is located. The substitute will be paid at the same hourly amount normally given to the secretary.

8. As the church grows it is expected that the secretary will become a full-time employee with benefits.

9. These regulations must be approved by the church board and placed in the minutes of the regular board meeting.

Basic Responsibilities

Filing
- Numerical by date (newest or latest date on top)
- Sort and move previous year to separate file drawer except legal items
- Use own judgment on where things go

Typing
- Visitors letters - Mondays
- Agendas, minutes, immediately after meetings
- Bulletins by Thursday
- Newsletters - 1st of the month
- Birthday and anniversary cards monthly

Mailing List
- Keep adding and revising

Phone Calls
- Screen calls
- Provide pertinent information to those who respond to advertising
- Take messages

Office Account
- Keep records of office account
- Quarterly report on income and expenditures
- Use for postage, office supplies, etc.

Calendar
- Reminders to pastor of appointments
- Special events outside church and church events

Work Assignments
- Must be approved by pastor; the secretary works for the pastor who will assign tasks.

Office Supplies
- Maintain an ample supply of materials for desks and equipment.

OFFICE PROCEDURE AND ORGANIZATION

An efficient filing system, calendaring of events, publishing of communiques and coordination of ministry schedules is of utmost importance.

A Filing System. In this section you will find a sample of one kind of filing system. There are many kinds, but suffice it to say, the adoption of a system will save the pastor, his staff and the office personnel much valuable time.

A Monthly Organizer Calendar. It is recommended that each office have a "year-at-a-glance" monthly organizer calendar which uses erasable marking pens. As you plan you easily get the big picture of what you expect to do in the coming 12 months.

Check Scheduling Dates. All ministry leaders should be instructed to check scheduling dates with the secretary and pastor prior to entering into specific planning. Overlapping often creates problems in the church. This is a major reason for weekly staff sessions.

SAMPLE FILING SYSTEM

No doubt there are many efficient filing systems which are adaptable to church administration. This outline is offered because many churches do not have any system. It may be expanded to greater length as the church and its ministries are developed. It is recommended that for easy reference a folder be developed which details the system.

THE NUMERICAL SYSTEM

1. LEGAL DOCUMENTS
- 1a. Constitution
- 1b. Church bylaws
- 1c. Charter/incorporation/tax exemption/insurance
- 1d. Official organization
- 1e. Membership (charter and letters of transfer)
- 1f. Deed and property documents
- 1g. Facility documents
   - 1g.1 - Lease (rental) agreement (mortgage), etc.
- 1h. Bulk mail permit

2. MINISTRIES
- 2a. Elders
- 2b. Deacons
- 2c. Deaconesses
- 2d. Nursery
- 2e. Sunday school
- 2f. Youth
- 2g. Ushers
- 2h. Women's Ministries
- 2i. Men's Ministries
- 2j. Music and Worship

3. ADMINISTRATION
- 3a. Advisory committee (church board)
- 3b. Annual meeting
   - 3b.1 - Nominating committee
- 3c. Financial reports
- 3d. Regional office

4. OFFICE
- 4a. Equipment service contracts
- 4b. Equipment manuals

4c. Petty-cash records
4d. Secretary - job description
4e. Previous calendars
4f. Correspondence
      4f.1. Visitor letters from church
      4f.2. Newsletters from church
      4f.3. Letters to/from pastors
      4f.4. Letters to/from regional office
      4f.5. Letters to/from denominational offices
      4f.6. Letters to/from others
4g. Catalogs
4h. Regional office newsletters/directives/programs
4i. Denominational newsletters/directives/programs

(As noted above this system may be expanded to great length.) You may want to design the categories according to the church needs and activities. But it is imperative that a filing system be designed and followed.

THE USE OF COMPUTERS IN THE CHURCH

by Dennis L. Gorton

Have you noticed lately how every Christian magazine is filled with ads pushing the use of computers in the church? Some of us have reacted and said it is just commercialization of the ministry and surely cannot be good for the Kingdom of God. If you are in that camp or if you really do not know whether or not the computer can help you, do me a favor and please read on.

SAVE MONEY AND TIME

I am convinced that this little gadget is one of the best things to happen to the church in decades. It can save you, the pastor, and your church many dollars as well as hours of time if used correctly. Here are some of the applications for computer technology in the church.

Word Processing

WORD PROCESSING is probably the first function of the computer that is applicable to the church. Notice the nifty bold capital letters at the beginning of this sentence. It is done by one touch of the button on the computer. Imagine how snappy your bulletin could be by using *one button italic*, **one button bold** and the other varieties of type available on the computer. Second, I have just made four mistakes in typing this sentence. They were easily corrected by just going back and typing over, deleting an extra letter or inserting a letter, all at the touch of a button. Because you are typing on a screen, not on paper, you save paper. You can toss your white-out, and give away your typewriter and its correcting tape.

The advantages of word processing for sermon preparation are innumerable. You can move paragraphs around, insert illustrations, delete material when the first time you preach the message it is 50 minutes long instead of 35, etc. You can also store all your messages on disks and save drawers of file space.

Your secretary, if you have one, will rise up and call you blessed when you give her a computer to work on. She will turn out twice as many letters in half the time, because she does not have to worry about mistakes or corrections.

Tracking Statistics

Keeping track of membership and attendance is a job that gets more and more difficult as the church grows. All programs of church software have a section for tracking membership and attendance. You simply enter the attendance data each week and ask the computer every week for a readout of those families or individuals who have missed two weeks in a row, and you have an instant visitation list. In addition to visitation, you can send out a computer-generated personal letter which can be individualized and personalized in half the time it would take on a typewriter.

Let's not forget about visitors. Every visitor who registers (in whatever way you do that in your church) will receive a personalized form letter in seconds by simply putting their names into the computer and merging the letter with the name of the visitor. This is the kind of personal attention, when followed up by a visit, that brings the visitor back again.

Tracking Finances

Financial records are difficult to keep, especially if you are in a church that has had a turnover of treasurers. It seems as if every treasurer has his or her own special system of bookkeeping that no one else can really figure out. The advantage of the computer is that it has a program tailored to your needs (because you buy the software program you need), and your treasurer then fits into the church's system and you have automatic consistency.

This is especially helpful to new or smaller churches that may not have someone trained in bookkeeping systems. The computer program does all the work if you simply enter the figures in the right places. Your treasurer will also love the computer when he or she discovers that instead of spending hours at the end of each month doing a financial report for the church he or she can spend time with his or her family instead. You ask why? It is simple. Once again the computer does the work of adding up the data and simply fits it into the correct report forms you have asked for. This takes minutes rather than the hours it takes to do this work by hand.

I hope by now I have convinced you that with a computer you can save a great deal of time, do better quality work and have more time to play golf—whoops! The computer typed that, not I! There are actually several more applications of the computer to church ministry, but these three basic uses should convince you that **YOU NEED A COMPUTER.** I would write about these other applications, but I am on my way out the door to play golf—this crazy machine! You just can't trust it once it gets to know you!

ESTABLISHING THE SUNDAY SCHOOL
AND CHRISTIAN EDUCATION MINISTRIES

NURSERY

FIRST IMPRESSIONS

The nursery is one of the most important ministries in your church. Young families need to be assured that their little ones will be carefully and lovingly cared for. When they bring the baby or toddler to the nursery door they look for a number of things:

- What kind of a person will be caring for their children?
- Does the attendant in charge seem to know what he or she is doing?
- Are there planned activities for their children?
- Are the toys clean, safe and orderly?
- Is the nursery itself clean and neat?
- Is there a system in place to contact the parents should a need arise?

These first impressions always reflect on the entire church.

NURSERY STANDARDS

Many people decide either to keep coming or to never come again because of what they see in the nursery. Therefore, we have developed the following standards for the attendant and the nursery room itself:

- The nursery attendant must utilize good Bible stories with pictures and other visuals to teach children up to three years of age. The Sunday school superintendent will provide direction and advice. The time during all services is to be used to teach the children. This is not simply a baby-sitting job; it is a ministry to little children. As the church develops the nursery should be divided into a nursery for infants to one year, and toddlers one to three. Three to five should have a pre-school program.
- The nursery attendant must dress modestly and yet in a practical manner in keeping with working with children.
- It is very important that the nursery attendant arrive at least 15 minutes prior to all services in order to receive early arrivals.
- The following items are a check list for the nursery attendant to follow:

Nursery Check List

1. Meet parents at the door and introduce yourself to them. Wear your name tag. Take the child in your arms or lead by the hand. Let the parent know

their child will have the best of care and attention. At their first visit have the parents complete an information form on their child. Keep it on file (see page 77).

2. Ask the name of each child and immediately write the name on a name tag. Make large black letters, using a marking pen. Use tape, not pins, to attach the tags.

3. Provide a game or toy to immediately occupy the child.

4. When the parents leave the child in your care, give them a copy of the Nursery Information paper. You should design this according to your own situation. Basically it tells how your nursery is operated, who is in charge and the purpose statement.

5. Be most careful to change diapers and keep the children clean. The attendant-in-charge should keep a good supply of disposable diapers.

6. Have juice and cookies available, but limit the amount to each child. It is the responsibility of the nursery attendant to purchase juice and cookies. However, the church should reimburse for them. Be sure to present all receipts when you make a request for reimbursement. (Coordinate with the Sunday school on how money is to be handled.)

7. Each Sunday after services, the crib sheets, cloths and towels should be cleaned in preparation for the coming week. Never use more than once.

8. Do not allow any children to leave the nursery without their parents.

9. Be sure all toys are safe, clean and very neatly stored.

10. Dispose of broken and/or dangerous toys.

11. Prepare a list of needed supplies and give it to the Sunday school superintendent. For example: Pampers, handiwipes, sealed wastebasket, cribs, sheets, specific safe toys, etc.

12. The church will attempt to recruit helpers to assist the attendant on a rotating basis in recognition that it is difficult for one person to handle all the children from infants to three years of age.

13. Only Christian books and music, approved by the Sunday school superintendent, are to be used. Dispose of all others.

   • Use action stories, simple drama that is short and full of conversation.
   • Use real-life objects to illustrate the Bible story.

- Workers should demonstrate the Bible truths in their own life.
- Use learning aids which appeal to the senses.
- Use the Bible itself.
  (1) Hold it while you tell the story so the children can see the connection.
  (2) Be reverent in attitude toward the Bible.
- Repetition is very useful for this age.

JOB DESCRIPTION FOR THE NURSERY ATTENDANT
(Sample)

1. The attendant must be an individual who loves children and is trained in the care of infants and children up to three years of age.

2. The attendant must be willing to receive training and supervision. The nursery and all its affairs come under the Sunday school superintendent.

3. The attendant must be able to teach the children Bible stories at their level of understanding.

4. The attendant is responsible for the well-being of the children. They must not be allowed to leave the nursery.

5. Changing of diapers and cleanliness of the children is of utmost importance.

6. The cleanliness of the nursery is the direct responsibility of the attendant. After the nursery is closed the attendant will vacuum the floor, clean the furniture, close windows and shut off the lights.

7. The toys must be cleaned with disinfectant after the nursery is closed. This may be done by dipping them in a tub of disinfectant and drying them with a nursery towel.

8. The sheets and other cloth items must be washed weekly.

9. All suggestions and reports must be submitted to the Sunday school superintendent.

10. The nursery attendant may be paid for her services. She will be paid hourly for that which is over and above the regularly scheduled program. A time sheet must be kept and given to the Sunday school superintendent, who in turn will submit it to the church treasurer.

NURSERY INFORMATION FORM
(Please Print)

Date _____

Name of child_____

Date of Birth _____ Sex : Male/Female

Parent Name_____
Circle one: Mother   Father   Guardian

Parent Address _____

_____

_____

Phone _____

Child's Personal Information:

Allergies (list any known):_____
_____

Special Concerns:_____
_____

Special Needs: _____
_____

Special Instructions: _____
_____

May your child have refreshments?_____

_____
                              Parent/Guardian Signature

Date: _____

Your signature disavows the attendant and church of all legal responsibility
in the event of a health problem involving your child.

THE CHILDREN'S CHURCH

The primary purpose of children's church is worship. Therefore, it must be properly organized and conducted. There are many different patterns for this group, but above all, definite steps should be taken to see that the spiritual needs of the children are met, that their relationship with the Lord is strengthened and that they are equipped in how to worship God.

It is recommended that from the very first public worship service a children's church be activated. Due to limited workers, this may not be easy. However, in church planting it is critical. Young families are often attracted to new churches because of the opportunities to serve. However, they want to be certain their children are cared for.

Often the church planter's wife will be the one to lead the way in establishing children's church. Regardless of who begins the program, the leader should always be training others to lead. Any Christian bookstore can provide the church with an abundance of children's church materials. Be creative and design the program according to the needs of the new church.

HOW TO START A SUNDAY SCHOOL

by Daryl Dale

The extension church must offer the children and young people of its congregation four ministries:

WORSHIP
INSTRUCTION
FELLOWSHIP
SERVICE OPPORTUNITIES

The Sunday school is often the means used to offer children and young people instruction and fellowship, but an extension church is often short of people who can teach Sunday school classes. If a church cannot offer the children and young people of its congregation worship, instruction, fellowship and service opportunities on a level these younger members can appreciate, it can be questioned whether the church has a right to serve them. Therefore, a lot of questions pertaining to Sunday school arise:

(1) WHEN DO WE START A SUNDAY SCHOOL?

The answer is simple: you start a Sunday school when you have teachers who can make the Sunday school both enjoyable and beneficial to the children and young people.

(2) WHAT DOES AN EXTENSION CHURCH DO WHEN IT CANNOT FIND TEACHERS?

It is not necessary for a church to start a Sunday school during its first few months of ministry. However, it is important that the church be able to explain to parents how the church plans to provide the worship, instruction, fellowship and service opportunities necessary for the spiritual growth of their children (i.e., a special worship program for children during, but separate from the adult worship service).

(3) HOW DOES AN EXTENSION CHURCH PROVIDE WORSHIP, INSTRUCTION, FELLOWSHIP AND SERVICE OPPORTUNITIES FOR CHILDREN AND YOUTH WITHOUT A SUNDAY SCHOOL?

Let us examine the needs of young people first. Young people can worship with adults beneficially if the services are less formal and choruses are sung as well as hymns. When a pastor's messages are filled with stories and illustrations, teens can benefit as much as adults. Teens can be part of an adult Bible class. They can also be given devotional workbooks to complete at home and bring to church.

Occasionally, the pastor or an elder can take the young people on a two-day retreat or to a Bible-teaching conference for intensive Bible study. Fellowship can best be provided by regularly taking your teens to a neighboring church for social activities. This may mean driving a number of miles once a month, but teens must have fellowship with other Christian teens.

Christian service opportunities in abundance can be provided to young people by the extension church. Reading Scripture, ushering, office chores, nursery supervision, special music, etc., can all be done by teens as well as adults.

Meeting the spiritual needs of children is also possible through the extension church. Perhaps Sunday school is not possible, but what about children's church or a Sunday or Wednesday night Bible club? Worship can be partially obtained by purchasing children's tapes which can be checked out of the church library. Fellowship needs involve social activities with just one or two other children. Bowling, picnics, fishing, visiting a museum, etc., can be done by a caring adult taking the children. Christian service opportunities are available to children through special programs at Easter, Thanksgiving and Christmas, such as passing out flowers on Mother's Day or May Day, or by making gifts and delivering them to shut-ins.

The extension church's ministries to children and youth must be written out so they can be given to visiting families. Most families are looking for a church with a Sunday school, but if you can meet the needs of their children apart from the Sunday school, parents will be impressed. The goal of starting a Sunday school when qualified teachers are available should also be stated in your church's literature.

(4) HOW DO YOU START A SUNDAY SCHOOL?

A Sunday school must have at least three classes: preschool children, school-age children and adults. Teens can attend the adult class or assist with the children's classes. Teen helpers must be involved in a Bible study program before they can be helpers in Sunday school. A home reading program would qualify as a teen Bible study program. Children under two years of age would be in a nursery or toddlers' class rather than a Sunday school class. The addition of new classes depends upon natural age-groupings and the actual number of students within each age group. Here is a chart which illustrates how to divide by natural age groupings:

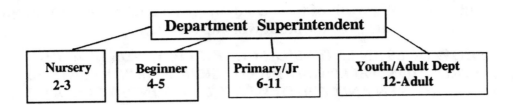

Department Superintendent			
Nursery 2-3	Beginner 4-5	Primary/Jr 6-11	Youth/Adult Dept 12-Adult

If there are two rooms which are used for classes, these should become departments which can utilize the whole Sunday school hour. Such a department may begin with as few as five pupils.

Primary (age 6)
Primary (age 7-8)
Jr. girls (age 9-11)
Jr. boys (age 9-11)
Supterintendent
Secretary
Pianist

Jr. High girls (age 12-14)
Jr. High boys (age 12-14)
Senior High (age 15-17)
Young Adult
Men's Class
Women's Class

Notice how the first new class or department added to the three basic divisions is created by dividing the nursery and beginner-age children. Both of these classes should be using a published curriculum and doing a considerable amount of Bible teaching.

Dividing grade-school children into classes for primaries (grades 1-3), and juniors (grades 4-6) can be done when the children's department reaches an attendance of 12. Youth can be separated from the adults when a church has four teens who regularly attend Sunday school.

Be careful of the danger of waiting too long to divide a class. Sometimes a teacher is not skilled enough to build a class to a dividable size. If you have qualified teachers, you might divide when you have 3-4 per class.

(5) HOW DOES THE TEMPORARY BUILDING AFFECT THE SUNDAY SCHOOL?

Buildings will influence the development of your Sunday school. It is very important that preschool children have a separate room. They tend to wander. If they are not contained by four walls their cries will be heard throughout the church and the teacher will have to constantly monitor their wanderings.

A large open room can serve the needs of the rest of the Sunday school. However, the open room must be divided with movable room partitions. Quality room partitions are expensive, but they are an excellent investment. Partitions are colorful, sound absorbing, moveable and useful as bulletin boards.

Some extension churches have purchased an enclosed trailer to house their partitions, tables, and chairs during the week. This equipment will be well utilized once an extension church has its own facility. The equipment you buy in starting a church will generally last 20-30 years. It pays to buy quality equipment.

The diagrams below indicate how portable dividers may be placed to create classroom space in one-room facilities.

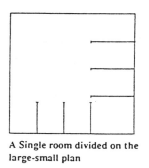

A Single room divided on the large-small plan

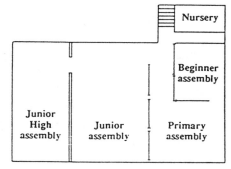

(6) WHAT GUIDELINES SHOULD BE SET UP FOR TEACHERS?

Job descriptions and guidelines are very important. The patterns you set up in starting a Sunday school will affect the quality of the Sunday school and establish it as a ministry of quality or a ministry of necessity. Quality is what you want people to think of when they refer to your Sunday school. Here are some general guidelines for Sunday school teachers:

GOALS FOR THE TEACHER

1. That each student should be saved and be growing in his or her love for the Savior.

2. That each student enjoy the class.

3. To increase the size of my class by personally visiting visitors, phoning absentees, prospecting and encouraging students to bring friends.

4. To be the best teacher possible, to influence lives for Christ.

TEACHER RESPONSIBILITIES

1. Attend all teacher's meetings.

2. Prepare each lesson well.

3. Bring visuals to class each week to illustrate the lesson.

4. Pray for each student more than once a week.

5. Phone each student the week after his or her first absence.

6. Read books on teaching.

7. Be faithful to the church and the pastor.

(7) HOW DO WE TRAIN NEW TEACHERS?

The best training is done by having the new teacher observe a gifted teacher on Sunday morning. Second, have each new teacher complete a Teacher Certification Program. Another good idea is to annually purchase one book on teaching for each teacher. Have the teacher write out a short report on the book.

Finally, if there are any Sunday school conventions in your area, take a carload of teachers to these motivational events.

(8) WHAT CURRICULUM SHOULD WE USE?

Curriculum choices are often difficult for the extension church. Teachers generally want to use the materials they utilized in their previous church. We would recommend that the extension church purchase Scripture Press curriculum from Christian Publications. Christian Publications has a program where extension churches can receive their first quarter of this curriculum free. (Certain limitations apply.)

Publishers will attempt to sell you many curriculum-related products. However, only four items are really necessary.

- Teacher's manual
- Pupil's manual
- Teaching-aid kit
- Flannelgraph correlated stories

Scripture Press publishes one teacher manual for each age group, but three pupil manuals. The pupil manual numbers can be interpreted as follows:

Primary 1 - first grade   Junior 1 - fourth grade
Primary 2 - second grade   Junior 2 - fifth grade
Primary 3 - third grade   Junior 3 - sixth grade

Select the pupil's manual that best represents the majority of your students. If you have combined primary and junior students, use either Primary 3 or Junior 1 depending upon which age-group comprises the majority.

(9) DO WE HAVE TO PURCHASE CURRICULUM MATERIAL?

Yes, if you believe your Bible study program should be systematic and purposeful. Experienced teachers often have a lot of miscellaneous teaching material in their closets. This material can be used for children's church, Wednesday night groups or on special occasions. However, the miscellaneous material will not provide your students with a solid Bible study program. Such materials are primarily evangelistic and do not meet the spiritual-growth needs of children who have already received Christ as Savior.

Establish the tradition of using a published curriculum in every class from toddlers to adults.

(10) WHEN DO WE NEED A SUNDAY SCHOOL CONSTITUTION AND THE VARIOUS COMMITTEES AND OFFICERS OF THE SUNDAY SCHOOL?

A Sunday school superintendent should be selected once you have three Sunday school classes. However, it is best if the extension church not fully organize its Sunday school until it has seven ongoing classes. Decisions can be made by the superintendent in consultation with the pastor or through gathering all of the teachers for a business meeting. Do not over-organize!

The second officer of your Sunday school should be a director of Sunday school outreach. This person's primary responsibility is to get the Sunday school to increase numerically. A description of this position can be found in the denominational manual.

(11) HOW CAN THE SIZE OF THE SUNDAY SCHOOL BE INCREASED?

Sunday schools grow in direct proportion to the number of people who are invited to attend. Therefore, promotion is the key to Sunday school growth. Invite 50 new people to your Sunday school every week and you will grow. Here is a list of some ways you can promote your Sunday school within the church and community:

- Periodic pulpit announcements
- Visiting all new residents to the community
- Offer free transportation to children and youth
- Distribute literature on the Sunday school throughout the community
- Contact prospective members through prospecting
- Obtain contacts through VBS or club programs
- Citywide mailing
- Door-to-door canvassing
- Sunday school contests

A printed brochure describing your Sunday school program should be distributed to all new residents and church visitors. It should be part of the package the pastor gives to church visitors when he goes to their homes.

ESTABLISHING VARIOUS CHURCH MINISTRIES

Every new church will have a unique community or area in which they are developing their ministries. Always ask, "Who are the target people? Are they young married, single adults or older people whose children are grown?" Knowing clearly your target group will be of utmost importance as you design your ministries. It could very well be that a nursery or a teen outreach may not be the first priority. On the other hand, these might just be the most critical things you could do. Be sure to have a clear picture of your ministry strategy before proceeding.

MINISTERING TO ALL AGES IS A MUST

1. **The nursery** should be open and staffed from the first service. A competent high school student or an adult person can be hired for a small fee each week.

2. **The children's church** is very important. Training must be provided for those interested in developing this ministry.

3. Immediately develop **a junior and senior high school ministry** through the use of sponsors.

4. **Young marrieds, young career, mid-adult and senior-adult ministries** can be developed with little effort.

5. The extension pastor must spend special time thinking through and researching these ministries. The district will provide the training if needed.

THE ANNUAL MISSIONS CONFERENCE

The annual missions conference goes beyond merely being a denominational event. It is the highlight of the year! This is the time when new people really catch the vision of what the global mission is all about!

The effective planning for a successful missions conference is most critical. Therefore, two outstanding manuals are available for the pastor and for your missions committee. For a small fee they are readily available. See the Index for ordering information.

ADULTS

As you dream and plan for future ministries be certain to include the many diverse groupings of adults. Single and career, the 30s and 40s with children still at home, the 50s and 60s who are seriously planning for retirement and, of course, the retired adults who have a lifetime of experience and wisdom to offer their church.

You might be surprised how many adults will enthusiastically work with you in developing a ministry unique to their needs. Use the Information Questionnaire included in this manual (page 107) to help discover these gifted individuals. Continually emphasize: "There is a ministry for every Christian of every age grouping!"

The more small-group ministries, the better. You will be amazed how a small group will grow and then must be divided again and again—thus keeping the growth momentum going! Do not be afraid to share ministry. These adults can do many of the typical "pastoral" ministries, so let them!

WOMEN'S MINISTRIES

It is wise for the women of the new church to prayerfully plan to organize the ministry as soon as the church is started.

Women's ministries are known for developing the very best annual missions conferences. Thus it is suggested that the pastor immediately establish special planning meetings with the group well in advance of the annual missions conference.

Always be searching for ways to allow the women of the church to reach their friends for Christ. Breakfasts, luncheons, teas and dinners with special attractions are good ways to reach out to many women. Be creative and do not be afraid to step outside the usual activity. In addition, be certain to maintain the wonderful missionary ministry of helps which is so greatly needed in global evangelism.

MEN'S MINISTRIES

The men of your church can have a very substantial ministry of helps both at home and overseas. Not only should the new church immediately form a men's group, but also begin to reach the men of the community through their programs.

One interesting and successful way to reach men is through a major monthly breakfast meeting. We are aware of a church with a record of successful evangelism to men which invites a well-known personality, not necessarily a Christian, to come as the keynote speaker. However, the men also carefully select a man with a strong testimony to share what God has done in his life. In addition, they usually invite another person with outstanding singing ability and clear testimony to sing one or two songs. With a program of this nature the men easily invite their buddies to come to hear the keynote speaker. They also hear a powerful testimony and meet other Christian men as well.

Always be creative and on the lookout for unique ways to give your men a chance to share their faith with their friends.

THE YOUTH

This includes young people from junior high through college. They need to have ministries to suit their particular age group, so determine to provide them with what is needed!

Pray that God will give you youth sponsors for each level. If you do not have anyone when the church first begins, you should set up a special time for youth and invite a para-church leader to come and speak, or show a Christian film. But by all means, start a youth program!

No doubt, as the church grows, you will have a youth director. However, often a volunteer director can be recruited from a local college. Many Christian students desire a ministry, but you may have to go in search of them! Trust God to provide, but do not sit back and simply wait. Begin immediately to search creatively for youth sponsors.

Families need and expect this ministry in the new church. It is amazing how many people come in the front door and go out the back simply because of lack of ministry for their children!

MONTHLY DISTRICT CHURCH-PLANTING REPORTS
ACCOUNTABILITY

You may be asked by those over you in the Lord to complete report forms. Accountability is something we all need.

One of the major items which should be examined regularly by those over you has to do with conversions and baptisms. These are very strong indicators of how the church is developing. The pastor must be taking the lead in evangelism. Of course, if there are conversions, then baptisms will naturally follow.

If people are not being won to Christ quite regularly, then it would be wise for the church planting pastor to reevaluate his ministry. Perhaps he has either not been trained or is not actively pursuing the excellent evangelistic training available, such as Evangelism Explosion.

A SAMPLE STATISTICAL REPORT

Statistical information assists us greatly in evaluating how we may help and advise you. Please do your best to give us a clear picture of your church.

Today's date _____

Name of church or group _____
Name of community _____
Circle one: Extension Church/Redevelopment Church/Extension Bible Study

The local pastor or leader will be responsible for preparing and sending the report. Please send by the tenth of each month.

Send the following with the report:

1. Copy of Advisory Committee or Governing Board Minutes
2. Copy of Monthly Financial Report

CHURCH MINISTRIES
Sunday A.M. Average Attendance_____ Baptisms _____
Sunday P.M. Average Attendance _____ Conversions _____
Midweek Average Attendance _____ New Members _____
Home Bible Study Attendance _____ Pastoral Visits _____

Other ministries: (VBS, clubs, police or hospital chaplaincy, Evangelism Explosion, radio program, other. List and report on each.)

_____
_____
_____
_____
_____
_____
_____
_____

PUBLICITY AND ADVERTISING: (Yellow Pages, newspapers, radio spots, brochures, other. List and report on each.)

_____
_____
_____
_____

To properly assess your *personal* and *church needs* we need to have as much information as possible. Please complete each category.

MINISTRY NEEDS

PASTOR AND FAMILY (monetary, housing, clothing, transportation, etc.)

_____
_____
_____
_____
_____
_____

CHURCH NEEDS (Supplies, equipment, etc.)_____

_____
_____
_____
_____
_____
_____

SPIRITUAL NEEDS OF THE CHURCH_____

_____
_____
_____
_____
_____

GENERAL COMMENTS OR SPECIFIC REQUESTS_____

_____
_____
_____
_____
_____

A SAMPLE FINANCIAL REPORT

EXTENSION CHURCH FINANCIAL REPORT

Please send this form, along with the monthly extension church report, to your regional office each month. Please put all items on your report although you may be using a computer or other means.

Monthly Financial Report

The Month Ending:_____ Year _____

Name of Church _____Date Sent In _____

City and State _____

Cash carried over (checking account only) $_____._____

        Cash in all savings accounts $_____._____

INCOME (ALL SOURCES)

Tithes and offerings: $_____._____

Designated gifts (list) _____ $_____._____

                 _____

                 _____

Building Fund $_____._____

Missionary giving $_____._____

Subsidy $_____._____

Other income (list) _____

                 _____

                 _____

TOTAL INCOME FOR THE MONTH: $_____._____

TOTAL ALL FUNDS ON HAND: $_____._____

EXPENDITURES

Pastor's Support $ _____._____ Review each December
FICA _____._____
Housing Allowance _____._____
Utilities Allowance _____._____
Phone Allowance _____._____
Auto Allowance _____._____
Health Insurance* _____._____
Church Rental or Mortgage_____._____
Advertising _____._____ 10% of Budget recommended
Printing _____._____
Office Account—Misc. _____._____
Fellowship Fund (1/2%-5yrs.) _____._____
Regional Operating Budget_____._____
Regional Extension Fund _____._____
Overseas Missions _____._____
Regional Pastor's Retreat _____._____ Savings
Regional Conference _____._____ Savings
Denominational Meeting _____._____ Savings
Other Expenditures (list)

_____   _____._____
_____   _____._____
_____   _____._____
_____   _____._____
_____   _____._____

TOTAL EXPENSE $_____._____

BALANCE LAST DAY OF MONTH OF _____

                       $_____._____

*Health Insurance is not to be considered as part of the pastor's support package.

THE ANNUAL REPORT

(for Denominational Churches)

If your denomination is like The Christian and Missionary Alliance, at the close of each calendar year you will receive an Annual Report to be completed by you personally. Once completed you will send it to your district superintendent, who will carefully examine it and send a copy to your national office.

The Annual Report will ask questions about your church; thus, it is most important to maintain careful records of: weekly Sunday school attendance, weekly worship service attendance, weekly midweek and home Bible study attendance and all financial transactions

There will be a due date noted on the Annual Report. You must be very careful and faithful in completing the report, because this is a vital part of the overall picture of your denomination's ministry.

BULK MAIL AND ITS USES

The mailing list is the name of the game! The importance of *direct mail* as well as an *ever-growing church mailing list* cannot be overemphasized! Some have questioned its effectiveness, but it is probably your most valuable and useful communication tool.

1. DIRECT MAIL

First, be sure to obtain a copy of the "Resurrection Sunday Manual." This valuable manual will detail for you how to use direct mail to reach great numbers of people. Basically it deals with the mailing of a special letter to thousands of people inviting them to an Easter Sunday service. Of course, the idea can be used for Christmas, Mother's Day, Thanksgiving or other high-point church attendance days. See the Index for ordering information.

2. MONTHLY CHURCH LETTER

Second, develop a regular monthly letter to your church mailing list. Be certain to put every possible person on this list. Of course, not all will come to your church, some never will. But they can still help you if they are informed of your ministries. Note, this is a letter from you, the pastor, and not a church newsletter or calendar. It is a personal letter giving a broad overview, and in some cases, a specific report of what is happening. Be certain not to use "Christian" jargon. Just make it a positive, enthusiastic letter.

Businessmen, friends, relatives, other pastors, anyone you have met, should be on the list. Produce 12 letters a year, and you will be pleased with the results.

3. VISIT THE POSTMASTER

In order to obtain a Bulk Mail Nonprofit Permit, you must visit the local postmaster and ask him for specifics on what is required to apply. We suggest this approach rather then attempting to detail it here because postal services sometimes interpret the method a bit differently.

ADVERTISING, PUBLICITY, MEDIA

PASTOR: Follow this format using wide margins, double spacing and capital letters. Include a professional black-and-white photo of yourself and the meeting place. Also, provide the editors with packets of attractive, informative literature on your new church and denomination. Hand deliver to the Religion Editor of the local newspapers.

SAMPLE NEWS RELEASE

AT LAST! A FRESH, NEW CHURCH FOR YOU WHO ARE NO LONGER ACTIVE IN A LOCAL CHURCH!

THE TOPEKA COMMUNITY CHURCH WILL BEGIN PUBLIC WORSHIP SERVICES AT FRANKLIN HIGH SCHOOL AUDITORIUM, 310 JONES STREET, SUNDAY, JUNE 7, 1987, 10:30 A.M.

OUR NEW CHURCH IS EVANGELICAL AND COMMITTED TO HAVING HAPPY, UPLIFTING SERVICES, WITH RELEVANT, PRACTICAL AND POSITIVE MESSAGES WHICH WILL MEET YOUR DEEPER NEEDS. CHILDREN AND NURSERY PROGRAMS ARE DESIGNED AND IMPLE-MENTED BY SKILLED TEACHERS JUST FOR YOUR LITTLE ONES!

YOU ARE WELCOME HERE! YOU WILL ENJOY YOUR NEW NEIGHBOR-HOOD CHURCH. LET'S GET ACQUAINTED! PASTOR BILL JONES WILL BE EAGER TO MEET YOU. FOR DIRECTIONS PHONE 555-5555.

AD SAMPLES

The designing of attractive and eye-catching ads is very important. Observe what others are doing. Many churches have very innovative advertisements in which they promote a program that meets a community need. For samples contact the Office of Church Growth of The Christian and Missionary Alliance.

CHAPTER 4

Initial Church Growth
and Continuing Momentum

WRITING THE MISSION STATEMENT

The Church Mission Statement, Statement of Purpose or Philosophy of Ministry must reflect that which you intend to do, to provide and to accomplish in your community.

1. The pastor and his key leaders should set aside a generous amount of time to thoroughly pray and work through the vision God has given them for the new church.

2. The statement should first be capsulized in brief paragraphs, followed by an explanation.

3. The statement must be based upon the actual needs of the community and how your church intends to meet those needs.

   • It should be geared toward the kind of people—ethnic, cultural and economic—living in the targeted region.
   • It should take into consideration the church's present as well as perceived future ability to meet the identified needs.
   • The statement is the church's vision and plan of action to evangelize and disciple the community, the surrounding regions and on into the world. As they work on the document, the designers of the statement must constantly ask, "How may we, as a local church, fulfill the Great Commission at home and ultimately overseas?"

4. Generalities are necessary and helpful in providing the initial framework, but the statement must deal in clear specifics in order to be carried out.

5. The statement must address, among others, the following:

   • The actual—not just perceived—needs of the community, i.e., Are the

people economically distressed? Do they need food, shelter, clothing? Are they wealthy but isolated? What are the divorce statistics? Is there a serious crime problem? What is the ethnic and cultural makeup of the area?
- What would be the most effective method of evangelizing the people of the area?
- What location and facility will fit the people and area?
- What worship style and preaching will be most appealing?

6. The statement must identify how the church intends to equip believers for active ministry.

7. The statement must also identify the primary target group — Christians, the unchurched, or both.

8. The statement is the basic plan of action. It requires much time, thought and prayer in its preparation. It is foundational to a successful church. It starts and sets the tone and direction for the whole future of the new church. Will your church be evangelistic? Will it be a church that helps people who are hurting? Will it be a church that intends to fulfill the Great Commission locally as well as overseas? Will it be a reproducing church that is constantly evangelizing other areas through planting daughter churches?

9. The statement should outline your short, medium and long-range goals in clear and precise statements. Begin with six months and work up to at least five years.

When you have completed your rough draft, send it to your regional extension director for his input and suggestions.

It is of utmost importance that each church state the purpose for its very existence, along with the practical outworking of how it intends to arrive at its objectives and thus fulfill the Great Commission (Matthew 28:18-20).

SAMPLE MISSION STATEMENT

PURPOSE STATEMENT

It is our desire and commitment to fulfill the Great Commission locally and worldwide by the proper equipping of the body of believers through (1) expositional Bible teaching, (2) the thorough teaching of the spiritual gifts and (3) practical evangelism, in order that the people may be able to do the various works of ministry resulting in the growth of the church (Ephesians 4:11).

ATMOSPHERE

All aspects of church life should be a reflection of the living, loving Lord Jesus expressing His resurrected life in and through the individual Christian as well as the congregation collectively. A sense of awe, praise, worship, joy, unity, excitement and enthusiasm should permeate every level of church life. The atmosphere sensed and expressed by all will be "the Lord Jesus is in this place"!

THE WORSHIP SERVICE

The centrality of Jesus Christ must be the primary focus of every worship service through the clear and practical expositional preaching of God's Holy Word. Everything in the worship format must bring glory to our Lord, whether it be the singing of the great hymns of the faith, praise choruses, special music, instrumentalists, testimonies or any other feature. Freedom of worship expression which reveres Christ and is not uncontrolled or disorderly is encouraged. Teaching or emphasis on controversial and/or doctrinal subjects shall be the responsibility of the senior pastor. All others in the church shall refrain from pursuing this emphasis.

MISSIONS

The emphasis on missions is every nation. It must begin with the local church reaching out to its community, then radiating out to the state, country and the nations of the world. Missions must translate into practical evangelism, the equipping of the believers, and resulting in the sending out of church-planting pastors and missionaries to bring the gospel of Christ to the lost at home and across the seas. The vigorous planting of daughter churches without thought of competition, loss of people or loss of money is the most efficient and biblical way of implementing missions at home. All ministries of the church should be to these stated ends—whether children, youth or adults.

The senior pastor and his staff should model evangelism and church growth for the church through such specialized outreaches as the police chaplaincy, radio Bible teaching, the teaching of evangelistic home Bible studies and Evangelism Explosion. The undergirding of the missionary work of the church must begin with sacrificial prayer on the part of the pastor, his staff and the leadership of the church. Otherwise all the activity is nothing more than a clanging symbol [sic].

THE FUTURE

In the adoption of the mission statement it becomes incumbent upon the church and its leaders to establish definable, measurable, specific goals with accountability. This will ultimately state the purpose in fulfilling the Great Commission at home and around the world.

Continuing growth both spiritually and numerically will be the natural outcome of this form of obedience. Nowhere in Scripture does God put a numerical limit on the size of a church nor on the planting of daughter churches. To do so is to impose a human standard on that which our Lord loves and gave His life for, which is the body of Christ, the church. The most natural occurrence in the church of Christ is growth. Without growth stagnation sets in, resulting in death in all its insidious forms—boredom, lifelessness, emptiness, apathy and lukewarmness.

The Holy Spirit desires to bring glory to Jesus Christ. He does so through forgiven, cleansed, repentant, Christians who have said no to self and yes to the Lord Jesus, thus allowing the Holy Spirit to fill their lives with the resurrected life of our Savior. The result? Growth in all its healthy forms!

In a church permeated by the Holy Spirit there will not only be an expectation of the imminent return of Christ, there will also be a vision for today and the future! Our blessed hope is Jesus in our midst now as well as a joyous "even so, come, Lord Jesus"!

HOW TO EXPERIENCE CONSISTENT, CONTINUAL GROWTH

A personal testimony
by Fred King

Two questions most frequently asked of me by fellow pastors, sometimes expressed in different and varying forms, or disguised in a maze and multitude of other matters, but always the intent of the conversation boils down to: "How can my church experience consistent and continual growth?" "If you were the pastor of this church, what would you do to bring about quality growth?"

I have never met a pastor, scholar, theoretician or church growth expert who can claim to have an absolute corner on this fascinating subject, although our theological libraries are rapidly being filled with an array of "Here's how it is done!" books.

Lest this section be construed as another "How to" or "Finally, here is the ultimate answer," may we agree together that this is simply one man's experience? Granted, there are quite a number of pastors who have had similar experiences and will stand alongside in powerful agreement that these approaches to ministry have borne great fruit and resulted in significant, rapid and quality church growth. Growth which is soundly based in protracted prayer, powerful preaching, soul winning, ministry to the Body of Christ and discipleship is always our priority.

MY FIVE MINISTRY PRIORITIES

"HOW CAN MY CHURCH GROW AND WHAT WOULD YOU DO IF YOU WERE THE PASTOR"

I have pastored four very different but growing churches. Why did each grow? Why so many conversions? Why did so many Christians show up at our doorstep? Why such a high level of lay involvement? The more the two premise questions were asked of me the more I was forced to identify the most basic reasons.

I began to list numerous possibilities as to why the growth, but the list seemed so top-heavy, involved and too cumbersome. One day not long ago an extension pastor looked me in the eye, after having listened to me at great length on many different ideas on how to get his little church growing, and asked simply, "Will you please tell me what your most basic priorities would be if you were the pastor here?" That forced me to identify the reasons! They came out as "MY FIVE MINISTRY PRIORITIES." Granted, each item could warrant numerous subtopics and information details, but this is only an outline approach.

PRIORITY #1

Sacrificial Prayer

If you skip this section, don't bother with the rest! Our Lord put it clearly and who can improve on His words?

> Ask and it will be given to you; seek and you will find; knock and the door will be opened to you. For everyone who asks receives; he who seeks finds; and to him who knocks, the door will be opened. (Matthew 7:7-8)

Probably the wisest thing after that would be to pronounce the benediction rather than talking about MY FIVE MINISTRY PRIORITIES! However, having been asked to put these priorities in writing, please patiently continue with me.

I would like to be quite practical. I must assume you believe in prayer. Great! But allow me to ask you, "How often do you and your church leaders meet to pray for one another, the church people and specific needs of the church? Wednesday night? Saturday morning? Sunday just before the service? Occasionally? Rarely? Never?"

Prayer, my friend, is the secret of success. Success, not by human standards or values, but heavenly success in your church, in your life. Remember, man measures success by how big, how many, how rich, how nice and a dozen or so other "hows." Heaven's success is measured by our relationship with the Son of God. If that relationship is right and proper, everything else comes together and incredible blessing will ensue! It's simple, but true, that God has committed Himself to prayer, although He is the omniscient, omnipresent, omnipotent God!

THE LEEWARD EXPERIENCE

We were a band of young men starting a church (Leeward Community Church of the C&MA) in Pearl City, Hawaii. Lacking just about everything—especially experience—and through a maze of very real crisis situations surrounding the actual survival of the new work on a day-by-day basis, we were drawn to prayer. All other possible resources were gone. Prayer was our only hope. It is interesting how we wait until everything else is absolutely depleted before prayer becomes serious business!

We began to meet daily, early in the morning for prayer. None of the prayers were eloquent, but we were certainly together in prayer! I can tell you, that was when things really began to happen at the Leeward Community Church! We recognized we were in the midst of the battleground of a great spiritual warfare, and human methods of solving problems were not working. The Holy Spirit of God came upon that little band of men and God brought great answers and met our needs! God gave us new people, gifted and equipped to develop numerous ministries. The financial picture cleared up and the bills were paid. Home Bible studies for the unsaved sprang up everywhere. The church began to grow in a very significant manner.

I could tell you about the other three churches in which I have served, as well, when

God in power came upon a band of men meeting for prayer daily, early in the morning. In each case people kept coming to Christ and the church grew and grew. People who had been attending for years were astonished. They had never before seen this happen.

It is my firm, unmoving conviction that the absolute first priority, above and beyond all other considerations, is for the pastor, his staff, all the elders and/or board members, to sacrificially covenant before God to meet together in daily prayer, regardless of circumstances. Rarely have I heard of this occurring. But where it has, the Holy Spirit visited, and revival and refreshing came to the congregation, and exciting continual growth became the norm.

DAILY INTERCESSION

The new church will be busy designing, developing and implementing one new ministry program after another, and rightly so. However, without consistent corporate prayer it will just be another church with much activity and little spiritual life. Prayer is critical for real life!

THE PASTOR LEADS THE WAY

The pastor must take the initiative and lead in prayer. Churches that experience the most remarkable growth and conversions are those who meet for prayer on a daily basis.

PRAYER IS COSTLY

The early morning daily prayer meeting will cost something. *First,* it will cost the removal of the veil that we tend to hide behind. When we pray the masks come off, and we get honest with God and one another. *Second,* it will cost an extra hour or so of sleep as well as breakfast for some. *Third,* it will cost convenience and comfort. Remember Mark 1:35-37 when Jesus got up while it was still dark, left the house and went to a solitary place to pray.

PERSIST AND BE FAITHFUL

Sometimes a pastor will ask others to come and pray, but no one will show up. Remember what happened to Jesus in the garden? Yet the angels strengthened Him. The pastor must persist and be faithful!

THE RESULTS

The results are wonderful! Scripture says we are to "keep on praying and not grow weary." As you spend protracted time in prayer with your church leaders God will provide people and resources! After all, God has committed Himself to prayer and He wants us to do the same.

PRIORITY #2

Prayer-Backed Preaching

Think about it. In the greatest pulpits of the Christian era the preaching has been expository and Holy Spirit empowered. I believe that a major result of sacrificial prayer will be powerful preaching!

Check it out. Visit with any thriving church and you will usually find a man filled with the Holy Spirit and preaching with great conviction. And behind the scenes without fanfare is a committal of the pastor and leaders to sacrificial prayer. The people will tell you the preaching is the best! They are excited! Enthusiastic! Expectant! Why? Because they see God at work in their pastor. They hear God speaking through their pastor. They see God's Word literally come to life through his preaching. These pastors major on the majors—prayer and preaching!

Are you a good preacher? An adequate preacher? A convincing preacher? Are your messages well organized and all your points clearly defined? Do you properly deal with all the current events, fads and popular Christian positions? That's okay. But that's not the point. God wants you to get enthusiastically serious about preaching the Word *with power from on high!*

I like to tell new church pastors to begin with the book of Acts because it tells the fantastic story of the birth of the church! Regardless of where you begin in Scripture, preach the Word thoroughly and be practical! Preach with conviction from the Holy Spirit and that, my friend, will come only from a vast amount of time in prayer. Yes, daily prayer with your people, but also much daily prayer in your own closet (Matthew 6:6).

Preaching Emphasis

THE PREACHER IN HIS STUDY

The following quotes are from Dr. W.A. Criswell, a Baptist pastor in one church for 34 years:

> If I have one thing to tell a young preacher, it would be this: Keep the morning for God. Shut out the whole world and shut up yourself to the Lord with a Bible in your hand and with your knees bent in the presence of the holiness of the great Almighty.

> What will the people say if the pastor is unavailable in the morning? How would the church get along?

> My answer comes out of long years of experience. The people will praise God for the pastor who will spend time with an open Bible on his knees before the Judge of all the earth.

> On a pastor's first Sunday he announces that he is their servant and shepherd to care for their souls day and night. He then explains that the morning he keeps for Bible study, for prayer, for intercession, for preparation. In the afternoon he does the work of the church, such as visiting, answering mail, counseling, etc. In the evening he attends the meetings. But in the morning he asks the people to leave him alone that he might stay in the presence of God.

Any church honors a request like that. They will love the pastor for it and will help him keep those hours sacred. Then, when the preacher comes before his people, he does not preach out of bare necessity, but out of the overflow of his life.

What does the preacher study in those mornings? I have a very definite, pragmatic answer. Always preach through some book of the Bible—it is better to preach through a book of the Bible.

Too many preachers walk up and down in their study wringing their hands, crying: "What shall I preach? And where can I get the pertinent material I need?" I walk up and down in my study, but my cry is altogether different. I am afraid I am going to die before I have delivered the message that I see in God's Book. When the preacher is expounding a Bible book, his text is automatically stated. All he needs to do is find out what the text says and what it means to us today.

Ten thousand times are the people bombarded with what the politician says, what the psychiatrist says, what the psychologist says, what the editor says. But what we would like to know is: Does God say anything? What does He say? This is the assignment of the preacher.

Always have some great godly direction and purpose. Drive it home with all your force. Stand on the word of God and on the basis of the Lord's authority. Make your appeal. It may be for consecration. It may be for prayer. It may be salvation. It may be for ministry commitment. The Holy Spirit will work with you, and the power of God will rest upon you.

PRIORITY #3

Targeting the Unchurched

One of my concerns has to do with us pastors who are in a comfort zone of unreality. We tend to become insulated and isolated from real people. People who are hurting. People who are calling for help, acceptance and love.

In my denomination, The Christian and Missionary Alliance, we have a radical heritage in the person of A.B. Simpson. One of the major reasons he left his high-salaried, prestigious position at the 13th Street Presbyterian Church in New York City was because of the hurting street people. He mingled with the so-called unsavory types—alcoholics, dope addicts, prostitutes, immigrants and down-and-outers of every description. He did not have a stained-glass-padded-pew-potluck-church, and boring sermon mentality. Simpson met people in crisis and led them to a saving knowledge of Jesus Christ.

Many churches in the United States do not annually report a single conversion. Most others report a slim few.

COMPASSION FOR THE LOST

To the pastors of these churches I have a question. What are you doing? No. What are you not doing? Jesus was and continues to be concerned about lost souls. This is why He has set apart you and me. We are to be soul winners! May He give a compassion for lost souls.

LACK THE TOOLS

I believe many pastors really do want to be on the cutting edge of seeing people come to Christ, but they simply lack the "tools" as to how to effectively, efficiently do it.

STATUS QUO

Some continue the programs that were in place when they came to the church, or if it is a new church, simply develop programs they have seen in other churches. Obviously, many have not been productive, other than simply maintaining the status quo.

MODELING

I am also of the conviction that the pastor must first be a model if he wants his people to get moving. I therefore recommend that pastors serve as police chaplains or in some form of community service in order that they may put to effective use the excellent Evangelism Explosion or other evangelism training they have received. Let me explain why. It must be understood that the police chaplaincy is but one way to penetrate a community with the gospel. Regardless of the method employed, the pastor must set the example in evangelism.

POLICE CHAPLAIN

I served as a police chaplain for seven years in two different departments. My church saw numerous converts as a direct result of this outreach. The chaplaincy was a part of my pastoral ministry and not simply a respectable community service project. Through this ministry I became a model of effective evangelism to my people, which in turn inspired them to share their faith.

Police officers, civilian workers and people reached through a multitude of field cases filled many of the seats in the four churches I pastored.

CITY PASTOR

You see, a chaplain almost immediately becomes the "city pastor." He will be called on for many civic functions and be an official representative of the police department and city. His church will become well-known in the region, and doors of all kinds will be opened.

UNENDING OPPORTUNITIES

Usually, I rode along with another officer Friday nights, which is the time of the most activity. This accomplishes a few things. First, the chaplain will be developing friendships and trust with the officers. This often takes a fair amount of time, since police by nature and training tend to be suspicious. Second, as you respond to various calls, many will be crisis situations—giving the chaplain tremendous opportunities to share Christ as well as follow-up by his church elders.

RIPE FRUIT

I remember many domestic and crisis-intervention situations which led to whole family units and many individuals coming to Christ. Dealing with loved ones of the victims of suicide, accident or crime are just a few of the crisis situations in which people are prepared like ripe fruit for the gospel of Jesus.

PRODUCTIVE AND EFFECTIVE

Our early morning prayer meetings bathed these hurting people in loving prayer. God wants us to be out there where the people are. I know one thing—every home will eventually have a crisis. Question: "How are you going to get into a home with the good news just at that critically fruitful time?" The police chaplaincy is one very productive and effective way. A sample job description for a police chaplain follows this section. It may be used in presenting the ministry to a law enforcement agency.

A SAMPLE JOB DESCRIPTION POLICE CHAPLAINCY PROGRAM

by Earl Herring
Chief of Police
Piedmont, California

I. PURPOSE

A. To provide spiritual guidance and counseling to all members of the Police Department, and their families in a time of need. *Note:* It is not intended that the chaplain replace an individual's own clergyman.

B. To assist police officers and members of the community through a field ministry.

C. To provide spiritual guidance, counseling and comfort in times of crisis to anyone in the community, and to refer persons to the appropriate agencies to assist them with individual needs.

II. QUALIFICATIONS

A. The Chaplain shall be an ordained minister or priest.

B. Shall possess sufficient experience in pastoral and parish work to enable him to appropriately cope with the spiritual and psychological needs of members of the department and the community.

C. Must be willing to conform to department policy, general or special orders.

D. Must participate in all mandatory training and assist in department training as needed.

E. Must be willing to accept appointment as a reserve or regular police officer as required by the Police Department.

F. Must be willing to wear the full uniform of a police officer as directed by the Chief of Police.

III. UNIFORM

A. The Chaplain is authorized to wear the regulation uniform of the Police Department. It shall be provided by the Police Department.

B. Shall be issued a Chaplain badge and identification card.

C. Nothing on the uniform shall identify the Chaplain by denomination.

IV. APPOINTMENT

A. Appointment shall be made by the Chief of Police.

V. DUTIES AND RESPONSIBILITIES

A. The Chaplain shall be responsible directly to the Chief of Police.

B. Shall report to a Deputy Chief for general and normal assignments and instructions.

C. Shall be available on a 24-hour basis and the scope of the services provided are:

   1. Community relations, training and departmental relationships

      a. participate in recruit orientation.

      b. attend department graduations, promotions, retirements and award ceremonies, dinners, social events, etc., and be willing to offer invocations and benedictions.

      c. visit homes of relatives to offer counsel and comfort in case of death.

      d. visit various department elements for the purpose of getting to know employees on a personal basis.

      e. call upon watch commanders of Field Operation units for assignment to on-duty sergeants or beatmen (this enables him to meet more officers, and permits him to become more cognizant of the problems that officers are confronted with during their tour of duty).

2. Field services and assigned responsibilities

   a. the Chaplain shall make hospital and house calls in cases of serious illness or long confinement.

   b. conduct, participate in or attend funerals of active as well as retired members of the department.

   c. visit homes of relatives to offer counsel and comfort in case of death.

   d. counsel officers and staff regarding personal and special problems relating to marriage, home, children, finances, etc.

   e. develop such relationships with officers and staff that might enable the chaplain to foresee personal problems in the making and to deal with them before they become acute.

3. Notifications

   a. in the event of an emergency, personnel may communicate directly with the Chaplain for assistance. (Other requests may be made through the designated Deputy Chief, Department Head, or designated liaison Chaplain.)

   b. the Personnel Division shall routinely provide the Chaplain with all necessary information regarding illness or death so hospital visitations or other arrangements can be made by the Chaplain.

   c. the Chaplain may assist the department and coroner's office in making death notices to the next of kin. (This could be in regard to a homicide, suicide, accidental or natural death.)

4. Field Assignments

   a. the Chaplain may be asked to assist beatmen in dealing with domestic quarrels.

   b. the Chaplain may be asked to counsel or console persons who are confused or emotionally upset.

   c. the Watch Commander may call on the Chaplain to respond as a police officer or as a back-up should the need arise.

   d. the Chaplain is permitted to ride with any officer on any watch.

   e. officers are to inform citizens who are victims or involved in a crisis that a Police Chaplain is available to assist them.

VI. OPERATION OF CITY-OWNED VEHICLES

A. The Chaplain is authorized to operate city-owned vehicles for official purposes and shall comply with all regulations contained in the General Order entitled Police Vehicles.

B. Certain vehicles are available 24 hours per day, seven days a week.

C. A roster identifying members of the Chaplaincy Corps by name, religious affiliations, church telephone listings, radio call numbers and geographic area assignments shall be published and correctly maintained for the information of all personnel.

VII. COMMAND AND CONTROL

A. The Chaplain shall be responsible directly to the Chief of Police. He shall be administratively assigned to a Deputy Chief. His duties shall be coordinated by the Personnel Division.

B. The Chaplain shall submit reports of activities to the Chief of Police as required.

C. A roster identifying members of the Chaplaincy Corps by name, religious affiliations, church, telephone listings, radio call numbers and geographic area assignments shall be published and currently maintained for the information for all personnel.

VIII. SALARIES, COMPENSATION, BENEFITS

A. The Chaplain may be salaried as a regular Police Officer or receive funding from independent sources such as his denomination or a private foundation.

B. Compensation may be given in the form of a gas allowance if his vehicle is used on duty assignments.

C. The Chaplain may be assigned a fleet vehicle for permanent official use. The vehicle may be kept at the Chaplain's residence or his office.

D. The Chaplain may be given an Office in the Police Department with necessary secretarial assistance and equipment.

IX. STATUS AND RANK

A. The Chaplain may not be assigned a rank but simply be referred to as

"Chaplain."

B. The Chaplain may receive a special rank that corresponds to a set pay-scale should the Chaplain receive a salary from the Police Department.

PRIORITY #4

Radio Bible Preaching

TARGETING CHRISTIANS

Here is where we shift gears. The Police Chaplaincy has as its target unchurched, hurting people. The radio Bible teaching outreach has as its target the Christian community. It is understood that not all will be able to use this approach. First, some background:

Dr. Wendell P. Loveless has been called the "father of Christian radio," since he was the first radio Bible teacher at Moody Bible Institute. Dr. "Pop" Loveless was wheelchair-bound and yet very active. He went home to be with the Lord in October 1987 at 96 years of age. Upon retirement from Moody many years ago, Dr. and Mrs. Loveless moved to Hawaii, and soon came out of retirement to again become a radio Bible teacher on the Billy Graham radio station KAIM. In the early 1970s Dr. Loveless, an avid promoter of our new church, again retired due to the poor health of his wife of 50 years. It was quite a shock to me as a young pastor when Dr. Loveless asked me to take over his program "Songs and Sunshine." Of course I could not do it, but with his insistence he began to instruct me how to teach the Bible in front of a production-room microphone. So it was that I eventually became the radio Bible teacher for KAIM Radio, doing simple book-by-book, verse-by-verse Bible teaching on the air.

WHO RESPONDED?

The results were phenomenal. Committed Christians began to visit the church seeking out a place to express their ministry gifts as well as their desire to be in an atmosphere of expositional preaching and teaching. Quality believers began attending, some new to the city, others from certain older denominations that had drifted from the Word of God and some from the charismatic movement who had come to realize that God's Word could deepen their spiritual lives far beyond the often surface experiences.

Again, in Colorado Springs, Colorado, I taught Bible on the air, and, again, the results were the same. Quality, growing, Spirit-filled Christians ready and eager to express their gifts in a biblical manner caused in each situation an excellent foundation for the development of numerous ministries. Rather than simply becoming or remaining a small single-cell church we, even in our early stages, became multi-cell.

MOST PRODUCTIVE TIME

It has been my experience that the most productive time is between 7:00 and 8:00 a.m., Monday through Friday, and if possible, repeat the taped program mid-morning, thus ministering to two audiences. A caution—do not use the time for interviews, music or promotion of your church. Use it to teach the Word, and the response will be very gratifying.

MINIMAL COST

A visitor response may be noted within the first few weeks, but more often it takes a full three months before people begin to visit the church in notable numbers. I recommend that you attempt to place your program immediately following one of the popular nationally known radio Bible teachers. The cost frightens some churches, but keep in mind that it takes but a few new tithing individuals, who begin to attend as a result of the program, to cover the program costs. Also, make it a permanent commitment as opposed to a temporary trial program.

FEAR FACTORS

I have found that pastors fail to use radio Bible teaching for three reasons. First, they seem to have a fear of the microphone. Second, they seem to have a fear of the cost factors. And third, they seem to have a fear of the amount of time necessary for material preparation. In my opinion all three can easily be addressed.

The Microphone

The radio station will be delighted to train the pastor how to record, use a mike, voice inflections, etc., simply because it will enhance the overall quality of their station. All you need to do is ask for assistance. They may even recommend the kind and quality of recording equipment needed so you can produce the program in your own study or a small room fitted with acoustical items to deaden the echo. Willingness to be trained, plus producing your practice programs, will overcome the initial fears. Remember, you can redo a program as many times as you wish.

The Cost

The cost factor has been addressed, but suffice it to say you should plan to spend about $3,000 to cover the first three or four months, depending on the fees charged by the local Christian radio station. It should be noted that, generally speaking, many Christian stations are noncommercial and will not permit a local church to have a daily program. However, make the request and offer a monthly donation of $300 to $500! Usually it is the commercial Christian station that is most receptive. Remember, you have the right to negotiate the program price. Whenever you hear them playing music, they are losing money.

The Time

Time to prepare materials is a major roadblock to most pastors. However, this should never stop you. Use previous message series and divide them into 13-minute segments so it becomes a continuing series. It lends some anticipation to the program! Preparing special studies for the program is a productive and much better use of your time than typing letters, bulletins and running dozens of errands all over town. Use your time wisely and God will bless you. If requested, I will assist you in basic training to get started. But, whatever you do, get started.

THE FIVE-MINUTE PROGRAM

There is another highly effective use of radio which can be used effectively on either a secular or Christian station. Developed by Rev. Anthony G. Bollback, it has proven to be an outstanding approach. It is a five-minute Bible question-and-answer program that can be used twice, three times a week or even daily.

1. A daily five-minute radio program at driving time will provide more exposure than a half hour program once a week. It can be as effective as a 15-minute daily program.

2. Choose a name carefully and stick to it. The one I used was "Here Is the Answer."

3. Determine how you intend to use the five minutes and who you want to reach. "Here Is the Answer" was intended to be a program which answered actual questions of people.

4. The format opening was consistent each day. For example: "Hello, everyone, this is Pastor Bollback of Kapahulu Bible Church. I have an interesting question for today from Mrs. E.W. . . . " Make this very warm and friendly. You are building rapport with your audience and attempting to capture their attention.

5. Answer one question per program. There is only time for one if you say anything meaningful. Always identify it with someone who called in or who wrote in. That makes it authentic. Speak to that person and others will identify with the question. For example, "Well, Tim, that's my answer to your question." It also encourages people to call in their questions.

6. For a start-up program or at any time when you run out of questions have your congregation or even your family write out questions for you. Always be sure that you actually are answering a question from a real person or you will be deceiving the public. If it sounds unreal, you will lose credibility.

7. On some occasions you can alter the format if you run out of questions or want to highlight a special feature. For example, at missionary conference time, you can ask the question yourself be saying. "Did you know Missionary So and So from Zaire reported recently that . . . ?" Then go on and talk about what they reported and invite people to attend your conference. Keep it warm and homey—not just an announcement. Make it come alive. If possible say, "Last week I was talking with Rev. _____ of Zaire and he said . . . "

8. Sometimes you can use parts of your sermon to answer a question someone asked at church. You can say, "Last Sunday a young person asked me a very startling question after the morning message. Mary asked. . . ?"

9. Always answer relevant questions. There is no need to get bogged down with speculation. Questions which do not relate to real life and daily living should not be part of your program. People want to hear answers to real problems.

10. Always leave room at the end to give your church name and telephone number. Adding the address and listing service hours should be avoided, as that detracts from the purpose. If you capture people's attention, they will find your church. If you can regularly be at the phone following the program, tell people you will be there to answer questions, but be sure you are there.

11. A five-minute program is very demanding. You must prepare a script because the time is so limited. You cannot go overtime, nor can you be caught short of material. It pays off though, because you can pack a lot into those few minutes and people will remember what you said.

12. From my experience, people will soon recognize your voice or name in other places. They will come up to you and ask questions or make comments about the program. They will also begin to call in their questions or other needs. Your congregation will grow because people will come where they get answers.

13. Never divulge a person's identity or use personal and confidential information you may have from a telephone conversation. It is proper to change the person's identity to protect them from being identified. You can say, "A caller asked me a question the other day. I'll just call him Tom for this program."

14. Don't answer questions about other churches. Stick to the Bible. Be positive. Never criticize another church or denomination by name. You will alienate your audience. Stick to relevant questions. Some stations have a policy which forbids the use of the names of cults on the air. They might be forced to give equal time to that group if their name is mentioned. This applies to liberal churches as well. You can say, "There are some groups . . . "

15. Practice reading your script so that it sounds natural and animated. Be sure you know your speaking speed. That will determine how much you can write for the allotted time.

16. Pray for the impact on the community. Have your people pray regularly for the program. Report responses to the congregation. That will encourage giving to the support of the program. Have them inform neighbors and friends about the program. You can develop an extensive audience through this medium.

17. If the station likes your program and gets responses, they will advertise it free other times of the day. My station would frequently say, "Be sure to tune into this station at four o'clock today to hear Pastor Bollback of Kapahulu

Bible Church answer your questions on, "Here Is the Answer." Keep the station informed concerning the number of telephone calls or letters you get. Share good ones with them.

18. When you really get into this kind of programming, offer a tape of the week's programs to people writing in. You can also offer the script. You may want to put a small charge on these items. That will happen only when you start to talk about real issues that answer people's questions. Remember for every letter or response you get, there are at least 50 people who listen but will not respond.

19. Don't give up easily. It's hard work, but it pays big dividends.

PRIORITY #5

The Evangelistic Home Bible Study Method

DISCIPLING AND OUTREACH

Here is where the previous four priorities begin to come together, for there must be a practical avenue of discipleship which insures the development and maturity of those responding to the gospel. This is also most critical in structuring the many varied ministries of the developing church. In other words, home Bible study groups can serve three important functions as well as a multitude of others.

Boiling it all down, there are at the most fundamental level but two specific kinds of home Bible studies: the evangelistic home Bible study and the home Bible study for believers. It is important to always keep this distinction in clear focus or the studies could otherwise prove to be counterproductive.

THE EVANGELISTIC HOME BIBLE STUDY

Home Bible studies for those who have not yet made a decision for Christ are absolutely essential. As the pastor and others make contacts throughout their community, whether through the police chaplaincy or some other means, there must be an avenue to follow in discipling them.

"Church Planting Through Home Bible Studies" is a handbook which provides a step-by-step process for training teachers and establishing the studies. It is available for just a small fee. See the "Index of Helps" for information.

If churches would adopt this method of evangelism and discipleship they would experience dramatic conversion growth. This could possibly mean adjusting the Wednesday evening service, with having numerous studies for Christians and non-Christians, taught by the pastor and other teachers throughout the city. Again, be certain to differentiate between studies for Christians and those for non-Christians.

THE SPIRITUAL GIFTS

DESIGNING CHURCH MINISTRIES

The subject of spiritual gifts has often been the subject of controversy. As Dr. Keith Bailey states in his excellent book *Servants in Charge* (Christian Publications), "The gifts of the Holy Spirit are not religious playthings but rich provisions of His grace for the purpose of ministry. Ministry is synonymous with service. The only proper use of gifts is to glorify Jesus Christ by serving Him" (p. 87).

The following forms are samples of an informative survey which can be used in any congregation to discover those who desire to serve in the church. With proper, careful teaching on the spiritual gifts, churches often find an abundance of people desiring to serve the Lord according to their giftedness.

In this way the many ministries of the church may be staffed, thus allowing the programs to be designed according to people who deeply desire to serve.

DISCOVERING GIFTED PEOPLE
Information Survey

The information you place on this form will assist the pastor and the church in the following ways:

1. To get to know you as a person.
2. To obtain an accurate mailing list for newsletters.
3. To assist us in the publishing of a Church Directory.
4. To assist you and us in discovering your talents, skills, abilities and spiritual gifts.

The prompt completion of this form will geatly enhance the rapid development of the ministry of our church. Please ask your spouse, teen children and older to *each* complete a separate form.

PLEASE PRINT OR TYPE

DATE:_____

NAME_____
      Last   First   Middle Initial

ADDRESS_____
        Street and/or Apt.

_____
    City   State   Zip

HOME PHONE(_____)_____

DATE OF BIRTH_____/_____/_____
            Month   Day   Year

NAME OF SPOUSE_____
              Last   First   Middle Initial

SINGLE ☐   WIDOWED ☐   ANNIVERSARY DATE_____

NUMBER OF CHILDREN _____

If children are living at home, please complete:

NAME: _____DATE OF BIRTH:_____

_____   _____

_____   _____

_____   _____

YOUR PRESENT OCCUPATION_____/_____
                                                        Business Phone

YOUR FORMER OCCUPATION_____

SPECIAL TRAINING AND EDUCATION_____

SPECIAL SKILLS, ABILITIES, HOBBIES, SPORTS, INTERESTS:_____

_____

_____

_____

_____

Do you know your spiritual gifts? Please check the ones you are sure of. Please circle the gifts you suspect you may have but are not quite sure.

1. ☐ Teaching
2. ☐ Helps/Mercy
3. ☐ Administration
4. ☐ Leading
5. ☐ Governing
6. ☐ Giving
7. ☐ Encouragement
8. ☐ Knowledge
9. ☐ Wisdom
10. ☐ Faith/Vision
11. ☐ Discernment
12. ☐ Miracles
13. ☐ Healings
14. ☐ Tongues
15. ☐ Interpretation of tongues
16. ☐ Other gifts specifically listed in Scripture

☐ I would like to attend a class on the spiritual gifts.

Have you ever served or had experience in one of the following areas of church ministry? Please add additional comments or ministries if necessary. Please check.

Ministry	When?	Where?	Specifics
☐ ELDER	_____	_____	_____
☐ DEACON	_____	_____	_____
☐ DEACONESS	_____	_____	_____

Ministry	When?	Where?	Specifics
☐ BOARD	_____	_____	_____
☐ WORSHIP/MUSIC	_____	_____	_____
☐ SONG LEADER	_____	_____	_____
☐ SINGER, GROUP/CHOIR	_____	_____	_____
☐ INSTRUMENT	_____	_____	_____
☐ USHER	_____	_____	_____
☐ TEACHER	_____	_____	_____
☐ TRUSTEE	_____	_____	_____
☐ YOUTH LEADER	_____	_____	_____
☐ KIDS CLUBS	_____	_____	_____
☐ LIBRARIAN/BOOKSTORE	_____	_____	_____
☐ TREASURER	_____	_____	_____
☐ CHURCH SECRETARY	_____	_____	_____
☐ OTHER:_____	_____	_____	_____

☐ I would like to eventually serve the Lord in one or more of the above areas of ministry.

Please list:_____

_____

_____

You will not be asked to serve unless you so indicate, and then only after careful discussion with the pastor. Compatibility is vitally important in church work.

☐ I AM A MEMBER OF THIS CHURCH.
☐ I WOULD LIKE TO BECOME A MEMBER.
☐ I WOULD LIKE TO SERVE.
☐ I WOULD LIKE TO MEET WITH THE PASTOR FOR ADDITIONAL INFORMATION.

LIST OF EFFECTIVE CHURCH-GROWTH METHODS

FOR CHRISTIANS
- Equipping through spiritual gifts
- Daily radio Bible teaching
- Nationally known speakers
- Discipleship Bible studies

FOR THE UNCHURCHED
- Police chaplaincy
- Evangelism Explosion
- Evangelistic home Bible studies
- Lunches with businessmen

FOR BOTH
- Daily early morning prayer
- Practical preaching (expository)
- Personal invitation
- Personal helps seminars
- Direct mailings
- Radio PSA's
- TV spots
- Special emphasis events
- Yellow Page ads
- Newspaper ads
- Films
- Excellent family & Christian Education programs
- Excellent worship services
- Excellent facilities
- Telemarketing

GOD'S STANDARD FOR CHURCH LEADERS

Occasionally the church will need to add new elders to the board. The selection process is taken from Scripture and is thus very specific. For positions of leadership in all other areas of ministry in the church the same basic screening process should be followed. The following specification sheet is taken directly from Scripture.

From *When All Else Fails, Read the Directions*
By Bob Smith

SCRIPTURE	QUALIFICATION	EXPLANATION
Titus 1:5-9	(1) Above reproach	Not open to censure, having unimpeachable integrity.
	(2) Husband of one wife	A one-wife kind of man, not a philanderer (doesn't necessarily rule out the widowers or certain divorced men).
	(3) Having believing children	Children are Christians, not incorrigible or unruly.
	(4) Not self-willed	Not arrogantly self-satisfied.
	(5) Not quick-tempered	Not prone to anger or irascible.
	(6) Not addicted to wine	Not overly fond of wine, or drunken.
	(7) Not pugnacious	Not contentious or quarrelsome.
	(8) Not a money-lover	Not greedy for money.
	(9) Hospitable	A stranger-lover, generous to guests.
	(10) Lover of good	Loving goodness.
	(11) Sensible	Self-controlled, sane, temperate.
	(12) Just	Righteous, upright, aligned with right.
	(13) Devout	Responsible in fulfilling moral obligations to God and man.

	(14) Self-controlled	Restrained, under control.
	(15) Holding fast the Word	Committed to God's Word as authoritative.
	(16) Able to teach sound doctrine.	Calling others to wholeness through teaching God's Word.
	(17) Able to refute objections	Convincing those who speak against the truth.
Additional from: 1 Timothy 3:1-7	(18) Temperate	Calm and collected in spirit, sober.
	(19) Gentle	Fair, equitable, not insisting on his own rights.
	(20) Able to manage household	A good leader in his own family.
	(21) Not a new convert	Not a new Christian
	(22) Well thought of by outsiders	A good representative of Christ among non-Christians.
Additional from: 1 Peter 5:1-4	(23) Willingly, not under compulsion	Not serving against his will.
	(24) According to God (In some Greek texts)	By God's appointment.
	(25) Not for shameful gain	Not money-motivated
	(26) Not lording it over the flock	Not dominating in his area of ministry (a shepherd is to lead, not *drive* the flock).
	(27) As an example	A pleasure to follow because of his Christian example.
	(28) As accountable to the Chief Shepherd	Motivated by the crown to be gained . . . authority to reign with Christ.

YOUR CAREFUL STUDY OF THIS OUTLINE IS ENCOURAGED
PRIOR TO CONSIDERING SERVICE IN THIS CHURCH.

CHURCH OFFICERS

It is recommended that bylaws, based on the following, be designed by the board and adopted at the annual congregational meeting.

THE DEACONS

SELECTION

The deacons are nominated by the elders and elected by the church for a one-year term. They are not a part of the board of the church.

COLLECTION

The deacons shall be the custodians and distributors of the benevolent "helps" fund, which they shall collect from the body of believers the first Sunday of each month. They may collect these funds by positioning a deacon by each exit with an offering bowl labeled "BENEVOLENT FUND." This special offering may be also collected by the passing of trays. They shall be responsible for placing an announcement in the bulletin for the scheduled Sunday.

PRIORITIES

The "helps" fund distribution shall be held strictly confidential. No person, other than the pastor, shall know of this distribution. The priority of distribution shall be as follows: active members of this church who are in desperate need; those who attend, but who are not members; former members; Christians who do not attend, but who can demonstrate that their need is genuine; and non-Christians who have real needs, and who can demonstrate the need is genuine.

PROCEDURE

The deacons shall not make decisions or determinations regarding policy or procedure, beyond the detailed and specific guidelines of this paper and the bylaws of the church. If they have specific suggestions they may, in writing, submit the same to the pastor and the elders.

ORGANIZATION

The deacons, immediately after their election, shall meet to select a treasurer, financial secretary and secretary from within their own ranks. The pastor and elders shall appoint the *chairman* of the deacons.

STANDARDS

They shall have a heart-attitude of growing toward the scriptural standards as set forth in the "Specification Sheet for Leadership" on pages 111-112.

BASIC RESPONSIBILITIES

Other specific duties and responsibilities of the deacons:

- Report all needs and suggestions to the pastor and elders.
  Visit the sick, the shut-ins and others needing "helps" attention.
- The chairman may on occasion ask the chairperson of the deaconesses to assist.
- Coordinate with the efforts of the deaconesses regarding their various ministries.

COORDINATION

Plan semiannual combined meetings with the deaconesses for planning and prayer. An elder, appointed by the other elders to oversee, will be in attendance. He will report to the elders. This will help insure that proper coordination will occur in all the "helps" ministries of the church.

The deacons shall consist of not more than five men.

THE DEACONESSES

The deaconesses may work together with the deacons as a joint diaconate board in conjunction with the pastor. Duties, responsibilities and ministries will include, but not be limited to:

- Preparation of the communion table.
- Visitations in the hospital and in the home.
- Visitation follow-up of former members and visitors to the church within one week of the visit.
- Receive money from the general budget for flowers, cards, etc., for those who are hospitalized or for families during time of bereavement.

The maximum number of deaconesses shall be five. Each one shall serve a three-year term.

MAINTENANCE TRUSTEES

1. The trustees have the responsibility of building and grounds which includes, but is not limited to, the following:

   - Lawn and landscaping.
   - Paint and structure repair and upkeep (interior and exterior).
   - Parking lot improvements.
   - Parsonage repair if church-owned.
   - Scheduling workdays and recruiting workers.
   - Scheduling of weekly church-cleaning crews.

2. The trustees shall meet once each quarter for a walk-through examination of

the facility to determine the necessary repair work and improvements needed.

3. They will investigate repair and/or improvement costs of materials, obtain three or four bids for work which must be done by contract.

4. Repair work may be accomplished at any time without approval from the church Governing Board. However, all structural changes and/or improvements must be approved.

5. The trustees are expected to use good judgment in determining what is needed. In other words, the church "trusts" them to take care of the facility without coming to the church Governing Board for normal repair and maintenance.

6. The trustees will be responsible for scheduling workdays with the chairman, coordinating the times and dates not in conflict with other church activities.

7. They shall be responsible for recruiting people to assist on workdays and other special projects.

8. There will be a trustee checking account. A certain amount determined annually by the board will be deposited in the account monthly. The trustees will select a treasurer and financial secretary to maintain the books. A monthly financial report will be submitted to the church Governing Board.

9. The head trustee may be a contract employee of the church. The salary will come under review in December of each year.

THE USHERS

1. The ushers shall be men who earnestly desire to serve the Lord in the ministry of "helps" in the church.

2. They may also serve as greeters at the entrances and exits, before and after all services.

3. There will be a head usher, with two other ushers to serve as assistants in the event of his absence.

4. The ushers should carefully select teenage young men to assist them in both morning and evening services, thus expanding the number of men to assist.

5. During winter months the ushers for the morning services shall wear a coat and tie and be as uniform in appearance as possible.

6. The ushers must always be on hand at least one-half hour prior to all services. If the ushers are involved in Sunday school classes, they should excuse themselves one-half hour prior to worship.

7. All ushers must know how to operate the sound system, taping, movie projector, VCR and other multimedia equipment.

8. The ushers must ensure that visitors sign the guest book and complete a visitor's card. The head usher must see to it that the senior pastor personally receives all visitor's cards.

9. The ushers must use good judgment as to when people should be seated during a service. Always be very friendly and respect the desires of the guest as to where he or she would like to sit.

10. The ushers will be responsible for handling emergencies: a sick person, a disruptive person or group, a spilled offering tray or communion tray, etc. The head usher will take charge.

11. The head usher must be attentive to signals from the pastor.

12. The ushers shall monitor the temperature of the building.

13. The ushers are responsible for the locking and unlocking of the doors, as well as a quick survey of the facility, inside and out, before and after all services, including a quick check of the restrooms, to make sure all is in order.

14. Good common sense is mandatory.

15. Excellent training manuals on ushering are available at local Christian bookstores. See the Index.

16. Quarterly training sessions should be scheduled to prepare new ushers and update regulars on current and future church events.

LEGAL AND CONSTITUTIONAL MATTERS

It is important for the new church to be established legally correct from the start. The following section provides sample forms for regulation, incorporation and constitutionalization of the new church. The samples provided are specifically designed for churches in The Christian and Missionary Alliance. Each denomination should have its own forms. If none are available to you, feel free to adapt these forms. Simply substitue your denominational name wherever "The Christian and Missionary Alliance" appears.

You must be very knowledgeable of the current denominational manual. This is your guide which must be followed. In the manual you will find the constitution for churches.

Each church will develop its own bylaws. However, they must not be in conflict with the denominational constitution. A set of sample new church bylaws are included in this section as a guide in developing them for your church. Prior to adopting the bylaws, be certain to ask the regional office to examine and approve them.

MANUAL OF THE DENOMINATION

We cannot stress too strongly how important it is for the pastor and church leaders to be thoroughly familiar with the denomination of their church. The denominational manual contains the General Constitution, Bylaws, Auxiliary Constitutions and Legal Charter of the denomination supplemented by other legal actions.

Single copies of the manual may be ordered directly from the national office of the denomination.

REGULATIONS FOR DEVELOPING CHURCHES

Most denominations or independent churches will find the following "Regulations for Developing Churches" an excellent guide for designing their own regulations.

Preamble

The Christian and Missionary Alliance believes that the local church is the visible, organized expression of the Body of Christ and that the local congregation finds broader meaning and ministry in fulfilling its biblical responsibilities within the life and witness of the larger body of the denomination.

Each Christian and Missionary Alliance church is an integral part of the district and worldwide fellowship of the Alliance and is united in governance, fellowship and service to promote unity of faith in the fullness of Jesus Christ as Savior, Sanctifier, Healer and Coming King, and to facilitate the spread of the gospel at home and abroad under the guidance of the Holy Spirit.

A "developing Alliance church" shall consist of a body of believers that has adopted and adheres to the Regulations for Developing Churches, and which meets regularly at an established time and place under the direction of a leader appointed by the district for the purpose of worship, evangelism, edification and fellowship, with the objective of becoming a fully organized church of The Christian and Missionary Alliance.

These Regulations for Developing Churches have been adopted by the Division of Church Ministries, and each developing church of The Christian and Missionary Alliance shall be governed by the following regulations until it is organized under the Constitution for Churches as it appears in the Manual of The Christian and Missionary Alliance.

1. **NAME** - This church shall be known as the _____ of The Christian and Missionary Alliance.

2. **PARTICIPATION** - Qualifications for participation in the developing church shall consist of the following:

A. Confession of faith in Jesus Christ and evidence of regeneration.

B. Belief in God the Father, Son and Holy Spirit; in the verbal inspiration of the Holy Scriptures as originally given; in the vicarious atonement of the Lord Jesus Christ; in the eternal salvation of all who believe in Him and the eternal punishment of all who reject Him.

C. Acceptance of the doctrines of the Lord Jesus Christ as Savior, Sanctifier, Healer and Coming King.

D. Full sympathy with the principles and objectives of The Christian and Missionary Alliance and cooperation by systematic support of its work.

3. **ORDINANCES** - Baptism by immersion is recognized as a scriptural ordinance. The Lord's Supper shall be administered regularly.

4. **ADVISORY COMMITTEE** - An advisory committee, appointed by the District Extension Director for a duration of six (6) months, shall consist of the pastor, secretary, treasurer, assistant treasurer and such other members as he may appoint. They shall be amenable to the District Extension Director. It shall hold monthly meetings for prayer and business and shall report to the district quarterly or as the district may direct.

5. **OFFICERS** - The officers shall consist of the following who, with the exception of the pastor, shall be appointed annually by the District Extension Director: pastor, secretary, treasurer, assistant treasurer.

6. **PASTOR** - The pastor of the church shall be appointed by the District Superintendent/Ethnic Director in consultation with the District Extension Director. He shall be under the supervision of the District Extension Director and amenable to the District Superintendent/Ethnic Director. The pastor may resign from the church by giving due notice of his intentions to the District Superintendent/Ethnic Director. The District Superintendent/Ethnic Director may ask for the resignation of the pastor in consultation with the District Extension Director. In consultation with the advisory committee, the District Extension Director shall determine the pastor's support.

7. **ELDERS** - Provided there are men meeting the requirements for eldership, a committee of no less than two elders shall be appointed by the District Extension Director upon the recommendation of the pastor. Elders shall assist the pastor in leadership and oversight of the spiritual ministries of the church. They shall, with the pastor and District Extension Director, constitute the committee on membership and discipline.

8. DUTIES OF OFFICERS

PASTOR - The pastor shall have general oversight of the work of the church in conjunction with the District Extension Director. He shall be chairman of the advisory committee and member ex-officio of all committees. When the church has no pastor, the District Extension Director shall have the oversight of the work and shall appoint an interim chairman of the advisory committee who shall preside at the business meetings.

SECRETARY - The secretary shall keep the minutes of advisory committee meetings and the membership roll, copies of which shall be given to the pastor and to the District Extension Director.

TREASURER - The treasurer shall receive all moneys of the church and shall pay all bills on the order of the advisory committee. He shall keep proper records of all transactions, maintain a record of receipts and present individual receipts to the donors. The District Extension Director shall determine where funds of the church shall be kept. The treasurer shall receive all missionary moneys and forward the same to the treasurer of The Christian and Missionary Alliance at the National Office on or before the 10th of the following month.

ASSISTANT TREASURER - An assistant treasurer shall be appointed who together with the treasurer shall count all moneys. He shall keep a separate record of all receipts.

9. **RECORDS** - The official records of all offices of the church and all of its departments are the property of the church. All financial records shall be audited annually or at any time on order of the District Extension Director. In the event of the death or resignation of the incumbent, or upon the appointment of his successor, the current records necessary for fulfilling the obligations of the office shall be passed on to the newly appointed officer. All records other than current shall be kept in a safe repository selected by the advisory committee.

10. **PROPERTY** - This church is connected with and subordinate to The Christian and Missionary Alliance, the parent religious denomination. Title to property, appurtenances and effects shall be held by the corporation of The Christian and Missionary Alliance within which jurisdiction this church is located or with which it is affiliated by law.

11. **GOVERNMENT** - The advisory committee shall conduct the affairs of the church and is amenable to the District Extension Director. There shall be a general congregational meeting held annually, at which time reports of all departments shall be presented, including audited reports of the treasurer. Notice of appointment of officers and members of the advisory committee

shall be given at this meeting, and all actions passed shall be subject to ratification by the District Extension Director.

12. **MISSIONS** - A missions conference shall be held annually for the promotion and support of the worldwide work of The Christian and Missionary Alliance. The church shall from inception give to the Great Commission Fund through the prepared Faith Promise Card supplied by the national office. These gifts shall each month be forwarded to the treasurer of The Christian and Missionary Alliance at the National Office.

13. **COMMITTEES AND ORGANIZATIONS** - Committees and organizations, as described in Article X of the Constitution for Churches of The Christian and Missionary Alliance, may be established as the need arises. Officers for these organizations shall be selected according to the following procedure: (1) the leader for the organization shall be appointed by the District Extension Director, and (2) other officers may be appointed by the advisory committee.

14. **DISTRICT FINANCES** - The church shall from inception give a district-regulated percentage of the monthly operating offerings to the District Operating Budget and to the District Extension Budget.

15. **FELLOWSHIP FUND** - Newly established churches shall pay a minimum of fifty percent (50%) of the normal church contribution for the first five (5) years (Board of Managers 1987). (See Fellowship Fund Regulations in the current Manual of The Christian and Missionary Alliance.)

16. **OFFICIAL ORGANIZATION** - A developing church with at least 20 adults who have completed a membership class, confessed Jesus Christ as Savior and Lord, and signed the C&MA application for membership may petition the District Superintendent/Ethnic Director to become an organized church. The Pastor and District Extension Director shall constitute the committee on membership in preparation for official organization.

   Readiness for organization shall be determined by the District Superintendent/Ethnic Director in consultation with the District Extension Director according to criteria defined in the Manual of The Christian and Missionary Alliance, the Constitution for Churches, and the district bylaws.

17. **AMENDMENTS** - These regulations may be amended from time to time by the Division of Church Ministries.

This agenda can easily be adapted by any church or denomination.

AGENDA FOR ORGANIZING AN ALLIANCE CHURCH

(Suggested Resolutions)

1. **Appointment of a Secretary Pro Tem.**

   Suggested resolution: BE IT RESOLVED that _____ be elected Secretary Pro Tem for this meeting.

2. **Resolution to organize a Christian and Missionary Alliance church.**

   Suggested resolution: BE IT RESOLVED that we, the following named persons, _____ , _____ , _____ , _____ , _____ having affixed our signatures to Application for Active Membership Cards for membership in The Christian and Missionary Alliance, a religious denomination incorporated under the laws of the state of _____ and of which Denomination District, incorporated under the laws of the state of _____ , is an integral part, do now organize ourselves as a local church of said Christian and Missionary Alliance.

3. **Resolution adopting an official name.**

   Suggested resolution: BE IT RESOLVED that this organization be known as _____ The Christian and Missionary Alliance, _____ .
   (city and state)

4. **Resolution adopting charter membership list.**

   Suggested resolution: BE IT RESOLVED that the persons named in Resolution #2 above shall constitute the charter Membership of The _____ Christian and Missionary Alliance, _____ .
   (city and state)

5. **Resolution determining closing date for charter membership.**

   Suggested resolution: BE IT RESOLVED that all persons completing the Application for Active Membership Cards for membership in The Christian and Missionary Alliance on or before _____ (date) shall be included on the charter Membership list of the church.

6. **Resolution for the adoption of The Christian and Missionary Alliance Constitutions.**

   Suggested resolution: BE IT RESOLVED that we adopt verbatim the constitution for churches, the Sunday School Constitution(s), the Alliance Youth Fellowship constitution(s), the Alliance Women local Constitution and the Alliance Men local Constitution, as approved by the General Council or the Board of Managers of The Christian and Missionary Alliance.

7. **Resolution determining the date of the annual congregational meeting.**

   Suggested resolution: BE IT RESOLVED that the annual meeting of the _____ (name of organization) shall be held _____ (date decided upon, which should take the following form, e.g.: "The first Tuesday after a Monday in the month of December").

8. **Resolution authorizing the chairman to appoint temporary officers and acting committees until the annual business meeting or a special congregational meeting is held.**

   Suggested resolution: BE IT RESOLVED that the chairman of the meeting be and is hereby authorized to appoint temporary officers and a temporary executive board. The said appointees shall serve until the congregation shall elect such officers and committee members at a congregational meeting.

9. **Resolution to authorize the inserting of the usual reversionary clause in all property deeds and church charter (Articles of Incorporation/Articles of Association).**

   Suggested resolution: BE IT RESOLVED that the church executive board be authorized to take any and all legal steps which are necessary for the insertion in all church property deeds and in the church Charter (Articles of Incorporation/Articles of Association) the following reversion clause of The Christian and Missionary Alliance:

   "The_____(name of church) is connected with and subordinate to The Christian and Missionary Alliance, the parent religious organization. Should this church cease to exist as a corporate body or cease to be subject to the purposes, usages, doctrines and teachings of The Christian and Missionary Alliance, then all its property, appurtenances and effects then owned or held by it shall revert to and become the property of the District of The Christian and Missionary Alliance within whose jurisdiction this church is located." "Should differences of doctrine arise between a church and the parent organization which do not yield to mediation, the reversionary provision may be waived by the following procedure: by two-thirds vote of the active membership of the congregation, by approval of the District Executive Committee, and by full consideration and approval of the Division of Church Ministries."

10. **Resolution to authorize the incorporation (or association) of the church according to the laws of the state.**

    Suggested resolution: BE IT RESOLVED that the church Executive Board be authorized to file Articles of Incorporation (or Association) with the Secretary of State of the State of_____.

11. **Resolution authorizing filing of copies of all official documents and minutes related thereto in the District Office.**

    Suggested resolution: BE IT RESOLVED that true copies of all official documents such as deeds, charter, mortgages and all official minutes related to these items, as well as minutes of this current organizational meeting, be prepared and sent to the district office for filing.

12. **Adjournment.**

MEMBERSHIP CLASSES

To be a member of the church, applicants should sign the membership card, share their testimony with the pastor and elders, who in turn vote on their acceptance. They are received into the church at the Sunday worship service or evening service. (Most pastors' manuals, available at local Christian bookstores will have examples of membership receptions).

Many a member does not understand the vision of the denomination, the centrality of the living Christ, the filling with the Holy Spirit and the missionary vision at home and overseas. If you plan membership classes, listed below are some areas you and your elders might want to cover:

1. See the constitution of the denomination.

2. The biblical plan of salvation and His Lordship.

3. The crucified life and being filled with the Holy Spirit.

4. Provide copies of the denomination's constitution and doctrinal statement.

5. Copies of the bylaws of the local church.

6. Explain why and how the local church was established and the spirit of the people.

7. Present the goals of the local church, growth, converts, the ministry to the congregation and current plans for the year.

8. The need for family worship, how to study the Bible, the desire to have the new members regular in all services and giving as practiced by the local church to meet the needs.

9. Encourage the new prospective members to seek to fulfill the "servant role" and not to seek power and authority.

10. Discuss the church's position on drinking, drugs, etc.

11. Discuss opportunities of using their gifts, talents and ministry in the church.

12. See that the church secretary keeps an accurate record of the membership, members received, date, transfers, etc. Christian bookstores will have a record book. In some churches elders are responsible to keep the membership records.

BAPTISMAL CLASS INSTRUCTIONS

It is assumed that baptism is preached and emphasized in the regular services of the church.

1. Distribute a tract or statement on baptism which is published either by the denomination or local church.

2. Explain what baptism signifies to the believer and should mean to each candidate.

3. Explain where and when your baptismal service will be held.

4. Explain the clothes they should bring with them for the baptism, and also towels and handkerchiefs, etc.

5. Be ready to share their testimony.

6. Explain how to stand when they are being baptized.

7. Have deaconesses and elders available to give towels when they come out of the water.

8. Give card out to be filled in for baptismal certificate.

9. See that the church secretary or elders receive information to place in their records.

SAMPLE NEW CHURCH BYLAWS

These bylaws can easily be adapted by any church or denomination.

TOLEDO COMMUNITY CHURCH
TOLEDO, OHIO

Bylaws

July 18, 1991

PREAMBLE

The New Testament teaches that the local church is the visible organized expression of the Body of Christ. It is therefore essentially a spiritual entity and best conceived of as a living, growing organism rather than as an expanding organization. Life is derived from the Head, Jesus Christ, on whom the church is absolutely dependent in order to be and to become all that God has called it to.

The people of God are to live and serve in obedience to the Word of God and under the Lordship of Jesus Christ. All believers have a vital role to play if the full ministry of the church is to be carried out. Each member of the Body must function as directed by Jesus Christ, the Head, and as empowered by His Spirit. This involves ministry: (1) to God—worship, (2) to those within the body of Christ—edification, and (3) to those outside the Body of Christ—evangelism. Overall leadership for these ongoing ministries is to come from the church board, a team of men chosen from among the local congregation for the godly quality of their lives as dictated by First Timothy 3:1-7 and Titus 1:5-9.

The local congregation finds broader meaning and outreach in fulfilling its biblical responsibilities within the life and witness of the denomination. As such, it is an integral part of the district and worldwide fellowship, and is united in governance, fellowship and service in order to promote unity of faith in the fullness of Jesus Christ as Savior, Sanctifier, Healer and Coming King, and to facilitate the spread of the gospel at home and abroad under the guidance of the Holy Spirit.

I. REFERENCE TO ARTICLE I - NAME

This church shall bear the corporate name of the Toledo Community Church of (denomination).

II. REFERENCE TO ARTICLE III - MEMBERSHIP

A. Application for Membership and Transfer of Membership

All applicants desiring membership shall meet with the church board or at least two representatives of such, and give testimony as to the saving power of Christ in their daily lives. Upon approval of the church board, they shall be accepted as members.

B. Baptism

Believer's baptism shall be strongly recommended to those seeking membership, as a necessary step of obedience in their walk with God.

C. Discipline

Any member having cause of complaint against another must seek to remove it according to Matthew 18:15-16 and Galatians 6:1. If this procedure fails to heal the breach, the issue will then be brought to the church board; a member guilty of conduct unbecoming to his Christian profession may be removed from membership, provided that reasonable notice of action has been given to such members, and opportunity provided for explanation. Individuals so removed may be readmitted to membership by applying in writing to the church board, receiving their approval, and by showing signs of consistent living.

D. Inactive Members

Members who are willfully absent from church services for a period of six months may be placed on the inactive list or removed from the membership list by recommendation of the church board. A letter stating such removal shall be sent. This transfer shall always carry with it the loss of privilege to vote in church meetings and to hold office in the church.

(1) Members who do not attend services for any of the following reasons may be placed on the inactive list and shall be automatically reinstated upon their return, provided they still meet the requirements for membership.

(a) Students attending college or school away from home.
(b) Those engaged in full-time Christian service, as pastors, evangelists, missionaries, etc.
(c) Those in military service.
(d) The aged, infirm or those residing in institutions or rest homes.

(2) Inactive members shall be contacted by the church board each year prior to the annual congregational meeting to determine their desire regarding membership.

(3) Persons placed on the inactive list may be reinstated by action of the church board upon proper written application, provided they still meet the requirements for membership.

III. REFERENCE TO ARTICLE V - GOVERNMENT

A. An annual business meeting will be held in the second week following the first Monday of January. The day of the week is to be selected by the church leadership.

B. Audited reports from the treasurer and others as determined by the church leadership shall be available.

C. One-third of the active members present at an annual or congregational meeting shall constitute a quorum.

IV. REFERENCE TO ARTICLE VI - GOVERNING BOARD

A. The church board and the elders shall be one and the same and as such shall perform all the functions of each board. All church board members shall be elected for one-year terms. Members may succeed themselves in office.

B. The maximum number on the church board shall be dependent, on the number who are scripturally qualified with a maximum of nine, including the pastor.

C. From these the church board shall select a secretary, a treasurer, a Christian education coordinator/Sunday school superintendent, and at least three trustees.

D. The church board shall be responsible for overall leadership and oversight of the church based on the principles of servant leadership found in First Peter 5:1-3; Matthew 20:25-28; and Matthew 23:10-11.

E. The church board shall appoint all committees deemed necessary. The church board may fill any vacancies that arise in elected offices. These appointed officers will then serve until the next annual election of officers.

V. REFERENCE TO ARTICLE X - COMMITTEES AND ORGANIZATIONS

Reference to Section 2 - Deacons

(1) There shall be a head deacon appointed by the church board to handle the Benevolent Fund and to respond to charitable needs as they arise as directed by the pastor and the church board.

(2) When needed, responsible men meeting the biblical standards shall be appointed by the church board to assist in the service ministries of the church.

Reference to Section 3 - Deaconesses

(1) They shall be appointed by the church board, who will determine their function and responsibilities. They shall serve under the direction of the pastor and the church board.

VI. REFERENCE TO ARTICLE XIV - ELECTIONS

A. The annual election of officers will be held in the second week following the first Monday of December. The day of the week is to be selected by the church leadership.

B. The nominating committee shall present the first reading of their report to the congregation at least three weeks prior to the annual election of officers. At least one name for each office to be filled will be presented. This will be presented in such a way as to fully inform the entire congregation. After this, individual nominations from the congregation may be presented in writing to the nominating committee. This committee, in consultation with the church board, shall determine the acceptability of these nominations based on scriptural qualifications and report to the congregation at the annual election of officers. The second reading of the nominating committee's report will then be presented at the annual election of officers.

VII. AMENDMENTS

Amendments to these bylaws may be adopted by a two-thirds majority vote of active members at the annual meeting or other congregational meetings. These amendments shall have prior approval of the church board and be posted at least two weeks prior to said meeting.

INSURANCE AND TAX EXEMPTION

The new church will function under the district guidelines until organized.
How to apply for the group umbrella of the Alliance.
When to apply for insurance in the new church.

Precaution to protect income of new church

The following direction was given by the CPA for The Christian and Missionary Alliance: that new, unorganized churches should take the following precaution to protect the money received.

On their checks and receipts of giving the following should be printed under the name of the church "of the District - C&MA." Such as:

_____of The _____ District - C&MA

If your checks are already printed you could have a suitable stamp made to identify it with the district. This means that until the church is organized, it is under the tax-exempt status of the district. When you are organized and incorporated, then application should be made for your church to be placed under The Christian and Missionary Alliance umbrella.

How a church can be included in the Group Exemption (tax umbrella) of The Christian and Missionary Alliance.

1. The first step is for the church to obtain a federal identification number. This is done by filing Form SS-4 with the Internal Revenue Service. The form can be obtained from the nearest IRS office.

2. When the district notifies the Division of Church Ministries at the National Office of the establishment of a new church, that church will then be added to the roster of churches. Letters will be sent to each pastor inviting them to become a part of the group exemption.

3. When the church completes the C&MA form containing the four questions* and returns it to headquarters, that church will be included in our next annual group exemption report to the Internal Revenue Service. A letter will then be sent to the church advising them that they have been included. This report is filed by October 1 each year.

    *The four questions are:
    •What is your corporate name?
    •What is your Federal Identification Number?
    •Is the church incorporated?
    •Has the church been organized and has it adopted the Alliance Constitution for churches?

4. The following January or February the National Office will send the church four copies of the Internal Revenue Service group exemption letter for its official records. This document states that The Christian and Missionary Alliance and its districts and local churches are recognized as tax-exempt organizations.

When should insurance coverage be secured?

It was generally agreed with insurance consultants that when a Bible study or worship services are started in rented facilities and the public is invited to attend, there should be liability insurance that would also include medical payments of at least $400-$500 per person.

1. It was felt that the homeowner's policy should give protection during the period of time the Bible study takes place.

2. When you move into rented facilities you may be asked about carrying liability insurance and should procure it as necessary.

3. When you organize and have a building, your liability insurance will be included in your total insurance package.

FORM OF CHARTER FOR CHURCHES
(Adopted by Board of Managers 9/85)

Certificate of Incorporation
of the
_____ (Name of Church)

We, the undersigned, _____ (A), _____(B), _____(C), _____(D), and _____(E), acting as incorporators of a corporation under the _____ (name of state) Statutes, Title _____ (if applicable), do hereby adopt the following Certificate of Incorporation for such corporation:

ARTICLE I.

The name of the corporation is _____ (name of church) of The Christian and Missionary Alliance of _____ (city and state).

ARTICLE II.

The corporation is a not-for-profit corporation organized and operated exclusively for religious purposes, is not formed for pecuniary profit or financial gain and no part of the assets, income or profits of the corporation is distributable to or insures to the benefit of its members, trustees or officers or any private person.

ARTICLE III.

The purpose for which the corporation is organized is to promote the cause of the Christian religion; to promulgate the doctrines and teachings of The Christian and Missionary Alliance, a corporation organized under the laws of the State of _____, with which this corporation is affiliated and connected as a subordinate body and should this corporation cease to exist as a corporate body in affiliation, cooperation or connection with the said parent corporation, viz., The Christian and Missionary Alliance, which has its principal office at _____, and subject to its purposes, usages, doctrines and teachings then all of the real and personal property, appurtenances and effects then owned or held by this corporation shall revert to and become the property of the incorporated or supervising body of The Christian and Missionary Alliance within whose jurisdiction said corporation is located or with which it is affiliated; to provide for its members a place of worship, to be conducted in accordance with the rules and laws of the aforementioned parent corporation, The Christian and Missionary Alliance of _____ (state); to receive, hold and disburse gifts, bequests, devises and other funds for its purposes, and to own and maintain suitable real estate and buildings for its purposes and do all things necessary and incident thereto.

ARTICLE IV.

The office of the corporation is to be located at (specify street address, city, village or town, county and state):

_____

_____

_____

The post office address to which the Secretary of State shall mail a copy of any notice required by law is (specify post office address):

_____

_____

_____

ARTICLE V.

Prior to the delivery of the Certificate of Incorporation for filing, all approvals or consents required by law will be endorsed upon or annexed hereto.

CERTIFICATE OF CONSENT TO INCORPORATION

of the

_____(Name of Church)

This instrument is to certify that on the _____ day of _____, 19____, _____ (name of church) of The Christian and Missionary Alliance, by and through its Board of Trustees, duly adopted the following resolution:

BE IT RESOLVED, that the _____ (name of church) of The Christian and Missionary Alliance incorporate pursuant to _____ (name of state) Statutes, Title _____ (if applicable), and pursuant to the purposes set forth in the Certificate of Incorporation.

On the _____ day of _____, 19____, said resolution was submitted to the members at a special meeting held at _____ (street address), City of _____, County of _____, State of _____, pursuant to notice as prescribed in the bylaws of the association.

At the aforesaid meeting, _____ members, representing at least two-thirds of all the members present at the meeting, voted in favor of the resolution to incorporate.

_____
Chairman

_____
Secretary

Signed, Sealed and Delivered
in the presence of

_____

ARTICLE VI.

This corporation shall conduct its business in accordance with the constitution for churches as set forth in the Manual of The Christian and Missionary Alliance as it may be amended by General Council from time to time.

ARTICLE VII.

The number of trustees selected for the first year of the existence of the corporation shall be three (3) and the name and street address of each trustee are:

NAME   ADDRESS

_____   _____

_____   _____

_____   _____

ARTICLE VIII.

The name and street address of each incorporator are:

NAME   ADDRESS

(A)_____   _____

(B)_____   _____

(C)_____   _____

(D)_____   _____

(E)_____   _____

IN WITNESS WHEREOF, we have hereunto set our hands this _____ day of
_____ 19_____.

(Signed) (A)_____

(B)_____

(C)_____

(D)_____

(E)_____

Signed, Sealed and Delivered
in the presence of

_____

STATE OF _____

COUNTY OF _____ SS

BE IT REMEMBERED that on _____(month, day and year), before me, the
subscriber personally appeared _____(A),
_____(B), _____(C),
_____(D), and _____(E), who, I am satisfied, are the
persons named in and who executed the within instrument, and thereupon acknowledged
that they signed and delivered the same as their act and deed, for the uses and purposes
therein expressed.

_____
(Notary Public)

THE BUILDING PROGRAM
WHEN TO BEGIN

BEFORE YOU BUILD

A number of congregations are spending thousands of dollars for extra architectural drawings that would be unnecessary if some careful precautions had been taken before you have an architect start preparing the working plans.

1. Write out the kind of church you are, how you worship and baptize, how the Lord's Supper is administered, the seating arrangement desired and the amount of room you envision in the new church.

2. Give information on the proposed site and that this is your first unit. It should include plans for additional sanctuary space and other needs of the congregation. Architectural plans should cover preliminary drawing of location on lot for additional building and how to connect it to present structure being considered. There is often the temptation to use the best site for the first unit and then there is difficulty working in the addition.

3. Write down the services held in a year: the morning worship service, evening service, Wednesday night prayer meeting and/or clubs, Bible study, women's or men's groups, executive committee, elders, the size and number of Sunday school classes, the space needed for youth work, pastor's study, church office, library, multipurpose room, size of narthex and any other special ministries of your group.

4. Scale growth of past five years, or projected growth, if a new church. Include attendance, finances, etc.

5. Call or write the district office for designs and plans from other churches which might be on hand.

6. Interview architects and see the designs they draw. Look at some of their buildings. Ask the cost for drawings. Also ask whether or not they would consider doing your drawings and let you secure the bids. Check with the clients that each of the selected architects has completed work for.

7. Stay in the preliminary stage until you have given considerable time to see that it is really what you need. Take them to the district office and the loan agency and have your first meeting covering a loan. Give the anticipated cost.

8. Plan your congregational meeting. Have the men who have helped plan the

design explain the building—where classes will meet and the size of the classrooms. You can have the preliminary drawings reduced to an 8 ½" x 11" sheet of paper and give them to each one to review.

9. Do your best to have a loan commitment before you order working drawings.

10. Working drawings should include the general as well as the mechanical and specifications. Every change you make on these will cost money.

11. Purchase the book "The Church Building Program." See the "Index of Helps" for ordering information.

HOW TO BEGIN

HOW TO LOCATE PROPERTY

In order to gain necessary information on a piece of property you should do the following:

1. Determine these things before going to a realtor:
   • Know the outside boundaries; i.e., what is the maximum distance you will go to plant a church (the region). Use a detailed street map.
   • Know the maximum price you will pay.
   • Know the size of land you want.

2. Find a realtor with a multiple-listing computer. He or she will provide a readout on every piece of available listed land in the area.

3. If the realtor fails to find something that fits your requirements then it is up to you. Do not make any commitments to a realtor. Tell him or her up front that you are using every available resource you can find. As far as realtors are concerned, first come, first served. They generally do not care for that, but remember, it is the Lord's money, and your church must set the guidelines. Also, by law, the realtor represents the seller, not the buyer.

4. If you locate a suitable property, visit the Bureau of Conveyances and the Tax Office. The clerks will show you how things work. You have the right to use these public records to find who owns a given piece of land. Many land owners are willing to sell but do not want to go through a Realtor or publicly advertise.

5. Know the Building Code and Land Use Regulations. You can purchase these from City Hall. It will cost a bit, but it is well worth it.

6. Check out the assumable mortgages first. The multiple-listing computer will

tell you just about anything you want to know.

7. Educate yourself on which lending institutions lend money on vacant land. Your realtor will know. Check with the district superintendent regarding the loan program of the denomination.

8. The site you want must have the following characteristics:
   - *Accessibility.* What are the main streets? Can you easily get to the property?
   - *Visibility.* Can it be easily seen?
   - *Size.* Does it provide excess parking? How large a facility can it contain when considering sanctuary, Christian Education, and parking? Your architect can calculate this.
   - *Terrain.* Is the land suitable to building? What special advantages and disadvantages does it have? Look at the positives.
   - *Zoning.* Obtain a copy of the Building Code and Land Use Code. Are you allowed to build a church here? Do you need a variance?
   - *Existing structures.* Can they be converted into church use? What is needed? Is it practical? What will it cost?
   - *Cost of land.* Have three or four realtors give you a market analysis. They can easily do this and should if they want your business. They simply check multiple-computer listings for what has recently sold and what is currently for sale. The listings must be similar to your preferred site. What terms are asked? Find how much the owner will negotiate the terms. Is there an assumable mortgage?

9. Compile all this information and be sure to list all your researched sites, beginning with the most expensive down to your preferred site. Note your specific reasons as to why this is the best possible site. Use a written statement by your realtor, attorney and other pastors in the area to substantiate your conclusions. Be sure not to exaggerate, but use facts and good "church location" sense. You must be completely convinced that this is the route to go. If you are not excited, convinced and demonstrating great faith, then do not expect anyone else to be convinced. You take the strong lead!

Land Evaluation Survey

Person making survey_____

    Address _____ Phone _____

    City _____State _____ Zip _____

Address of Site _____

Suburb or city _____

Name of Realtor _____

Owner of property _____

(1) Location:

        _____inner city

        _____residential

        _____suburb

        _____county

        _____other

(2) Zoning:

        _____residential

        _____agricultural

        _____commercial

        _____other

(3) Restrictions:

        _____one story only

        _____business

        _____industrial

        _____no septic

        _____no driveway access

(4) Easements:

    Water?   Yes_____No____   How many feet? _____

    Sewer?   Yes_____No____   How many feet? _____

    Electric? Yes_____No____   How many feet? _____

    Street?   Yes_____No____   How many feet? _____

    Other? _____

(5) Water bench: _____ feet.

(6) Flood area? Yes _____ No_____

(7) Set-back requirements:

    (a) from adjoining property _____

    (b) from the street _____

(8) Unpaid assessments? Yes _____ No _____ Amount: $_____

(9) Unpaid taxes? Yes _____ No _____ Amount $ _____

(10) Terrain:
    1. _____woody
    2. _____swampy
    3. _____needs fill Estimated yards _____
    4. _____level
    5. _____hilly
    6. _____other _____

(11) Available utilities:
    1. Sewer?   Yes____No____ Already in _____
    2. City water?   Yes____No____
    3. Electric?   Yes____No____
    4. Natural gas?   Yes____No____
    5. Fire hydrants?   Yes____No____ How far from site?_____

(12) Availability:
    1. Driveway?   Yes____No____ Already in _____
    2. Curbs?   Yes____No____ Already in _____
    3. Sidewalks?   Yes____No____
    4. Paved streets?   Yes____No____
    5. Off-street parking? Yes____No____

(13) Visibility:
    1. Corner site?   Yes _____ No _____
    2. Neighborhood?   Yes _____ No _____
    3. Freeway?   Yes _____ No _____
    4. Near public school? Yes _____ No _____
    5. Near a shopping center? Yes _____ No _____
    6. Near a railroad?   Yes _____ No _____
    7. Near an airport?   Yes _____ No _____
    8. Other? _____

(14) Soil:
    1. Test made?   Yes _____ No _____
    2. Suitable for foundations? Yes _____ No _____
    3. Suitable for septic system? Yes _____ No _____

(15) Accessibility:
    1. From freeway?   Yes _____ No _____
    2. From highway?   Yes _____ No _____
    3. From street?   Yes _____ No _____

(16) Natural barriers? Yes _____ No _____ If so, what are they?

(17) Artificial barriers? Yes ____ No ____ If so, what are they?_____

(18) Other churches in area:
     1._____
     2._____

(19) Legal:
     1. Attorney?   Yes ____ No ____
     2. Available title?   Yes ____ No ____
     3. Title insurance?   Yes ____ No ____
     4. Land survey?   Yes ____ No ____
     5. Plot plan?   Yes ____ No ____
     6. Engineer's elevations? Yes ____ No ____

(20) Include a map of the area marking schools, church, shopping center, etc.

Used Building or Church Evaluation

Person making survey_____
    Address _____ Phone _____
    City _____State _____ Zip _____
Address of Site _____
Suburb or city _____
Name of Realtor _____
Owner of property _____

(1) Location:
    _____ inner city
    _____ residential
    _____ suburb
    _____ county
    _____ other, explain _____

(2) Zoning:
    _____ residential
    _____ agricultural
    _____ commercial
    _____ other

(3) Restrictions:
    _____ one story only
    _____ business
    _____ industrial
    _____ no septic
    _____ no driveway access

(4) Easements:
     Water?   Yes_____ No_____How many feet?_____
     Sewer?   Yes_____ No_____How many feet?_____
     Electric?   Yes _____ No_____How many feet?_____
     Street?   Yes _____ No_____How many feet?_____
     Other? _____

(5) Water bench: _____ feet.

(6) Flood area? Yes _____ No_____

(7) Set-back requirements:
     (a) from adjoining property _____
     (b) from the street _____

(8) Unpaid assessments? Yes _____ No _____ Amount: $_____

(9) Unpaid taxes? Yes _____ No _____ Amount $_____

(10) Terrain:
     1. ____woody
     2. ____swampy
     3. ____needs fill   Estimated yards _____
     4. ____level
     5. ____hilly
     6. ____other _____

(11) Available utilities:
     1. Sewer?   Yes_____ No _____ Already in _____
     2. City water?   Yes _____No _____
     3. Electric?   Yes_____ No _____
     4. Natural gas?   Yes _____No _____
     5. Fire hydrants?   Yes_____No_____How far from the site?_____

(12) Availability:
     1. Driveway?   Yes _____ No _____ Already in _____
     2. Curbs?   Yes _____ No _____ Already in _____
     3. Sidewalks?   Yes _____ No _____
     4. Paved streets?   Yes _____ No _____
     5. Off-street parking? Yes _____ No _____
     6. Is parking adequate? Yes _____ No _____
     7. Is parking adequate for Yes _____ No_____
        future growth?

(13) Visibility:
      1. Corner site?   Yes _____ No _____
      2. Neighborhood?   Yes _____ No _____
      3. Freeway?   Yes _____ No _____
      4. Near public school?   Yes _____ No _____
      5. Near a railroad?   Yes _____ No _____
      6. Near an airport?   Yes _____ No _____
      7. Other? _____

(14) Soil:
      1. Test made? Yes _____ No _____
      2. Suitable for foundations for future construction?_____
      3. Suitable for septic system, if ever needed? Yes _____ No _____

(15) Accessibility:
      1. From freeway?   Yes _____ No _____
      2. From highway?   Yes _____ No _____
      3. From street?   Yes _____ No _____

(16) Natural barriers? Yes _____ No _____ If so, what are they?_____
_____

(17) Artificial barriers? Yes _____ No _____ If so, what are they?_____
_____

(18) Other churches in area:
      1._____
      2._____
      3._____

(19) Legal:
      1. Attorney?   Yes _____ No _____
         Name _____ Phone_____
      2. Available title?   Yes _____ No _____
      3. Title insurance?   Yes _____ No _____
      4. Land survey?   Yes _____ No _____
      5. Plot plan?   Yes _____ No _____
      6. Engineer's elevations? Yes _____ No_____

(20) Include a map of the area marking schools, church, shopping center, etc.

(21) Does the building have a bad reputation?

(22) What needed repairs will be required?

Estimated Cost

1. Footing_____
2. Walls _____ Inside _____ Outside _____
3. Painting_____ Inside _____ Outside _____
4. Flooring_____
5. Carpet_____
6. Roof_____
7. Windows_____ Inside _____ Outside _____
8. Other_____

(23) Has a professional builder or someone who knows buildings examined the property in consideration? Yes_____ No _____

(24) If yes, what is the evaluation? _____

_____

(25) Is there room for future expansion? _____

_____

(26) Are the facilities adequate to meet the:
    1. present needs? Yes _____ No _____
    2. future estimated needs? Yes _____ No _____

(27) Recommendation from person or persons making evaluation.

_____

_____

_____

(28) Has the district office been informed? Yes _____ No _____

WHEN YOU BEGIN

CHECKLIST FOR CONSTRUCTION

The following has been prepared for new churches planning construction. Please fill out in duplicate, one for your use and one to mail to the district office. The building plans must be approved prior to construction. Please send a copy of preliminary drawings for approval. Later when working drawings are complete, send a copy of them for the district files.

1. Cost of the land _____
2. Architect and soil engineer _____
3. Permits, extra sets of plans, bond, etc. _____
4. Excavation and grading _____

5. Landscaping and sod/grass _____
6. Parking lot (Check if blacktopping is required) _____

Cement Work

7. Footings and foundation walls _____
8. Basement floor _____
9. Precast floor system (if used) _____
10. Waterproofing _____
11. Sidewalk and steps_____

_____
_____
_____

Mechanical

12. Plumbing (interior) rough in and finish_____
13. Sewer or septic system, drain field _____
14. Heating plant (specify if oil, gas or wood)_____
15. Well or water lines from the street_____
16. Interior electrical material and labor_____
17. Exterior electrical material and labor_____
18. Allowance for electrical fixtures_____

_____
_____

General

19. Framing, studs, plywood, trusts, joists, siding, roofing_____

_____
20. Windows and exterior doors _____
21. Sheetrock, insulation, vapor barrier _____
22. Taping, spraying, ceiling _____
23. Nails and fasteners _____
24. Hardware, weather stripping, caulking _____
25. Interior trim, doors, casings, window trim, paneling_____
26. Kitchen cabinets, and other cabinets needed_____
27. Counter tops _____
28. Paint and stain _____
29. Vinyl floor coverings _____
30. Ceramic floor coverings _____
31. Allowance for carpeting _____
32. Bathroom partitions _____
33. Bathroom package (mirrors, wastepaper baskets, dispensers)

_____

Miscellaneous

34. Furniture, pews, pulpit, communion table, etc._____
_____
35. Hymnals, organ/piano _____
36. Tables, chairs for Sunday School and fellowship hall _____
37. Church sign _____
38. Fire extinguishers_____
_____

Subtotal $_____

Costs for labor not included in above_____
_____
_____
_____
_____

Total $_____

Please note:

- Be sure you have loan approval in writing and all required stipulations fulfilled before construction starts.

- Builders Risk Insurance should be secured before construction starts. It should also include volunteer labor, if there are areas you plan for volunteers to work on during construction. After the building is completed and a fire rate has been established, then change it over to a good multi-peril policy.

- Before construction begins, plan a meeting of all subcontractors and explain where the loan has been secured, how bills should be submitted and that there should be lien waivers for work done to the time a bill is submitted. This must cover all labor and material purchased for the church, which is purchased by contractor or subcontractor. Lien waivers may be purchased at an office supply.

FINANCING THE PROJECT

BULDING FINANCE PROGRAM

The Office of Church Growth of The Christian and Missionary Alliance sponsors a program to assist the local church in raising money from within the congregation. Do not miss out on this excellent program! Other denominations may also use the program.

ALLIANCE DEVELOPMENT FUND (ADF)

The Alliance Development Fund is an investment-savings plan whereby our people may invest their savings on a stewardship basis. Their money does double duty, earning interest for them as well as building new churches.

Money received from the above investments provides mortgage funds to qualifying churches applying for assistance in their building programs. Since many churches have difficulty in securing loans from commercial institutions, this fund becomes all the more valuable to them.

When it comes time for the church to secure a loan from ADF they must complete the application and submit it to the district office for processing prior to it going to The Christian and Missionary Alliance National Office. The district can provide the church with information and application materials.

NATIONAL APPLICATION GRANT REQUEST FORM

The National Church Growth Office endeavors to provide small grants to extension churches as the national budget allows. The church may ask the district office for the Application Grant Request Form. The form is self-explanatory.

INDEX OF HELPS

1. CHURCH GROWTH

The Church Growth Survey Handbook
Bob Waymine & C. Peter Wagner
A Global Church Growth Publication
25 Corning Avenue
Milpitas, CA

Activating the Passive Church
The Small Church Is Different
Getting Things Done
Growing Plans
Assimilating New Members
Lyle E. Schaller
Abingdon Press
201 8th Avenue S.
Nashville, TN

Your Church Can Be Healthy
Leading Your Church to Growth
C. Peter Wagner
Regal Books
2300 Knoll Drive
Ventura, CA

How to Build a Magnetic Church
Herb Miller
Abingdon Press
201 8th Avenue S.
Nashville, TN

Birth of the Body
Growth of the Body
Triumphs of the Body
Ray C. Stedman
Vision House Publishers
Santa Ana, CA

Ten Steps for Church Growth
Donald McGavran & Winfield C. Arn
HarperCollins Publishers
10 E. 53rd St.
New York, NY

Body Life
Ray C. Stedman
Gospel Light Publications
P.O. Box 3875
Ventura, CA

Prepare Your Church for the Future
Carl F. George
Fleming H. Revell Co./Baker Book House
P.O. Box 6287
Grand Rapids, MI

20/20 Vision
Dale E. Galloway
New Hope Community Church
11731 S.E. Stevens Road
Portland, OR

Multihousing Congregations
David T. Bunch
Smith Publishing
3049 West Roxboro Road, N.E.
Atlanta, GA

Beyond Church Growth
Bob Logan
Fleming H. Revell Co./Baker Book House
P.O. Box 6287
Grand Rapids, MI

Church Growth Strategies that Work
Donald McGavran & George G. Hunter, III
Abingdon Press
201 8th Avenue S.
Nashville, TN

2. CHURCH PLANTING

Church Planting at the End of the 20th Century
Charles L. Chaney
Tyndale House Publishers
P.O. Box 80
Wheaton, IL

Planting Churches Cross-Culturally
David S. Hesselgrave
Baker Book House
P.O. Box 6287
Grand Rapids, MI

The Church Planter's Training Manual
Fred G. King
Christian Publications
3825 Hartzdale Drive
Camp Hill, PA

Getting a Church Started
Elmer Towns
Church Growth Institute
P.O. Box 4404
Lynchburg, VA

Resurrection Sunday
VISION Weekend (with video)
Vision 94 (with video)
Church Planting through Home Bible Studies
Office of Church Growth
The Christian and Missionary Alliance
P.O. Box 35000
Colorado Springs, CO

Planter's Toolkit
Bob Logan & Steve Ogne
Charles E. Fuller Institue
P.O. Box 91990
Pasadena, CA

Church Planting Workbook
Church Planter's Checklist
Robert E. Logan & Jeff Rast
Charles E. Fuller Institute
P.O. Box 91990
Pasadena, CA

Church Planter's Manual
Harold E. Amstutz
Association of Baptists for World Evangelism
Cherry Hill, NJ

Missions Have Come Home to America
The Church Is in a Stew
Jerry L. Appleby
Beacon Hill
Kansas City, MO

The Principles and Practice of Indigenous Church Planting
Charles Brock
Broadman Press
Nashville, TN

Church Planting at the End of the Twentieth Century
Charles L. Chaney
Tyndale House Publishers
P.O. Box 80
Wheaton, IL

The Bivocational Pastor
Luther M. Dorr
Broadman Press
Nashville, TN

The Church Planters Handbook
Jim Durkins, Dick Benjamin, Larry Tomczak
   and Terry Edwards
Christian Equippers
Box 16100
South Lake Tahoe, CA

Church Planting for Reproduction
Samuel D. Faircloth
Baker Book House
P.O. Box 6287
Grand Rapids, MI

Stepping Out on Faith
Jerry Falwell and Elmer Towns
Tyndale House Publishers
P.O. Box 80
Wheaton, IL

Church Planting by the Team Method
James H. Feeney
Abbot Loop Christian Center
2626 Abbott Road
Anchorage, AK

Church Planting Methods
David E. Godwin
Lifeshare Communications
DeSoto, TX

How to Plant Churches
Monica Hill, ed.
MARC Europe
London, UK

On the Front Lines: A Guide to Church Planting
Joseph F. James
Free Methodist Church
Winona Lake, IN

Strategies for New Churches
Ezra Earl Jones
Harper and Row
San Francisco, CA

Thank God for New Churches
James H. Lehman
Brethren Press
Elgin, IL

A Practical Guide to Church Planting
Roger N. McNamara, ed.
Baptist Mid Missions
Cleveland, OH

Planting Growing Churches for the 21st Century
Aubrey Mulphurs
Baker Book House
P.O. Box 6287
Grand Rapids, MI

Antioch Blueprints
James Nikkel
Board of Evangelism
Canadian Conference of Mennonite Brethren
    Churches
Winnipeg Manitoba

Planting Churches That Grow
Opal L. Reddin
Central Bible College Press
Springfield, MO

Planting New Churches
F.J. Redford
Broadman Press
Nashville, TN

A Technical Manual for Church Planting
Duane Ruth-Heffelbower
Mennonite Board of Missions
Box 370
Elkhart, IN

44 Questions for Church Planters
Lyle E. Schaller
Abingdon Press
201 8th Avenue S.
Nashville, TN

How to Plant a Church of God
Bill F. Sheeks
Pathway Press
Cleveland, TN

Creating Communities of the Kingdom: New Testament
Models of Church Planting
David W. Shenk & Ervin R. Stuzman
Herald Press
Scottsdale, PA

Church Planting: Always in Season
Timothy Starr
Fellowship of Evangelical Baptist Churches of
Canada

Upon This Rock: Dimensions of Church Planting
William C. Tinsley
Baptist Home Mission Board

1350 Spring Street, N.W.
Atlanta, GA

Getting a Church Started
Elmer L. Townes
Privately published by the author

"How to Plant a Church" Self-Study Pack
C. Peter Wagner
Charles E. Fuller Institute
P.O. Box 91990
Pasadena, CA

Church Planting for Greater Harvest
C. Peter Wagner
Regal Books
2300 Knoll Drive
Ventura, CA

3. CHURCH MINISTRIES AND HELPS

The Christian and Missionary Alliance Resource Guide
Office of Communications
The Christian and Missionary Alliance
P.O. Box 35000
Colorado Springs, CO

The Pastor's Planner
Finance Manual for Alliance Church Treasurers
    (and Pastors)
Division of Church Ministries
The Christian and Missionary Alliance
P.O. Box 35000
Colorado Springs, CO

Communicating Missions - 2 manuals
    1. A handbook for the Missions Committee
    2. A handbook for Pastors
The Office of Missionary Deputation
The Christian and Missionary Alliance
P.O. Box 35000
Colorado Springs, CO

Growing Together
(A 6-week membership program for Alliance
    churches)
Christian Publications
3825 Hartzdale Drive
Camp Hill, PA

Church Usher: Servant of God
David R. Enlow
Christian Publications

3825 Hartzdale Drive
Camp Hill, PA

Servants in Charge
Keith Bailey
Christian Publications
3825 Hartzdale Drive
Camp Hill, PA

4. THE BUILDING PROGRAM

The Church Building Program
Building Finance Program
Raising Money for Capital Investment
Division of Church Ministries
The Christian and Missionary Alliance
P.O. Box 35000
Colorado Springs, CO

Church Property and Building Guidebook
T. Lee Anderson
Convention Press
Nashville, TN

5. EVANGELISM HELPS

One to One: A Practical Guide to Friendship Evangelism
Terry Wardle
Christian Publications
3825 Hartzdale Drive
Camp Hill, PA

Evangelism by the Book: 13 Biblical Methods
Tom Stebbins
Christian Publications
3825 Hartzdale Drive
Camp Hill, PA

Oikos Outreach
This is an evangelism curriculum you can use quarterly in your adult Sunday school classes. Designed to help Christians to reach their friends, relatives, neighbors and associates. Four new lessons to come out each year.
Tom Stebbins
Christian Publications
3825 Hartzdale Drive
Camp Hill, PA

"Personally Yours"
This is an eight-page, evangelistic, direct mail newspaper that churches can have sent to homes in their communities. The sponsoring church puts its name on the logo and also uses two pages each issue for information about itself.
Dr. William Goetz, editor
Christian Publications
3825 Hartzdale Drive
Camp Hill, PA